The Collegiate Learning Assessment

Setting Standards for Performance at a College or University

Chaitra M. Hardison, Anna-Marie Vilamovska

Prepared for the Council for Aid to Education

RAND EDUCATION

The research described in this report was produced within RAND Education, a unit of the RAND Corporation. Funding was provided by The Council for Aid to Education.

Library of Congress Cataloging-in-Publication Data

Hardison, Chaitra M.
    The Collegiate Learning Assessment : setting standards for performance at a college or university /
Chaitra M. Hardison, Anna-Marie Vilamovska.
        p. cm.
    Includes bibliographical references.
    ISBN 978-0-8330-4747-2 (pbk. : alk. paper)
    1. Collegiate Learning Assessment. 2. Universities and colleges—Standards—United States.
I. Vilamovska, Anna-Marie. II. Title.

    LB2367.27.H37 2009
    378.1'66—dc22

                                                                                            2009026700

The RAND Corporation is a nonprofit research organization providing objective analysis and effective solutions that address the challenges facing the public and private sectors around the world. RAND's publications do not necessarily reflect the opinions of its research clients and sponsors.

RAND® is a registered trademark.

Published 2009 by the RAND Corporation
1776 Main Street, P.O. Box 2138, Santa Monica, CA 90407-2138
1200 South Hayes Street, Arlington, VA 22202-5050
4570 Fifth Avenue, Suite 600, Pittsburgh, PA 15213-2665
RAND URL: http://www.rand.org/
To order RAND documents or to obtain additional information, contact
Distribution Services: Telephone: (310) 451-7002;
Fax: (310) 451-6915; Email: order@rand.org

PREFACE

This report describes the application of a technique for setting standards on the Collegiate Learning Assessment (CLA), a measure of critical thinking value-added at higher education institutions. The goal of the report is to illustrate how institutions can set their own standards on the CLA using a method that is appropriate for the unique characteristics of the CLA. As such, it should be of interest to those concerned with interpreting and applying the results of the CLA, including administrators and faculty at participating CLA institutions.

This research has been conducted by RAND Education, a unit of the RAND Corporation, under a contract with The Council for Aid to Education. Questions and comments regarding this research should be directed to Chaitra M. Hardison at chaitra@rand.org.

CONTENTS

TABLES

SUMMARY

The Collegiate Learning Assessment (CLA), produced and administered by the Council for Aid to Education (CAE), is an assessment of higher education critical-thinking skills. It consists of three types of constructed-response tests, measures a combination of high-level cognitive skills, and emphasizes school-level value-added in its reports.

Although institutional value-added, or how much students improve after attending college or university, is the primary method of CLA score reporting, it is not the only possible approach to CLA score interpretation, and some questions about CLA scores cannot be addressed with a value-added methodology. For example, many schools ask: Is a given CLA score considered "satisfactory" or not? This is akin to asking for a standard or benchmark against which to judge student performance; however, no such standard is provided in CLA score reporting. Because no such standard exists, the purpose of this report is to present evidence about the effectiveness of one method that schools can use to answer this question on their own.

As with any type of test interpretation, evidence of the reliability and validity of that interpretation is critical (AERA, APA, and NCME, 1999). We therefore assembled and examined evidence of reliability and procedural validity of a standard-setting methodology that we developed and applied to the CLA.

The standard-setting study we conducted included nine panels composed of 41 faculty from participating CLA institutions across the United States. The standard-setting method consisted of three steps. First, each panel member read answers arranged in order of score. For seniors and freshmen separately and without conferring with the other panel members, each panel member identified the range of scores that he or she felt represented performance at each of the following four standards: *Unsatisfactory/Unacceptable, Adequate/Barely Acceptable, Proficient/Clearly Acceptable,* or *Exemplary/Outstanding.* Second, in groups of four to five, panel members arrived at consensus within their group on the ranges of scores that represented the performance required at each performance standard. Third, panel members sorted a set of randomly ordered, unscored essays into each of the four categories.

The results of the standard-setting process were promising. Overall, the three standard-setting steps produced similar standards for performance on average; however, we did observe variability across individuals, panels, and different CLA test prompts, as well as high unreliability in the sorting process. Based on these findings, we recommend that institutions using this standard-setting method increase the number of panels, include multiple CLA test prompts, increase the number of responses used in the sorting step, and lengthen the time to complete the sorting step as an effort toward improving the accuracy and reliability of the standard-setting results.

ACKNOWLEDGMENTS

We would like to thank several people at the Council for Aid to Education who contributed to the research reported in this manuscript: Roger Benjamin, Dick Hersh, Marc Chun, Chris Jackson, and Alex Nemeth for their assistance in soliciting faculty nominations from CLA institutions for our standard-setting panels and coordinating the panels; Esther Hong for providing CLA responses for use in the standard-setting process; and Stephen Klein for providing feedback on the study and manuscript. We would like to acknowledge those at the RAND Corporation for their contributions as well: Brian Stecher for his feedback on the methodology, and Julie Ann Tajiri for her tireless efforts toward compiling and organizing the standard-setting materials and coordinating the standard-setting panel meeting in Santa Monica. We are also grateful to Barbara Plake and Brian Stecher, who provided thoughtful reviews of this manuscript; their comments led to several improvements to the final version of the document. Last, but not least, we would like to thank the 41 faculty who served as our panel members.

ABBREVIATIONS

ACT	ACT, a college entrance exam
AP	Advanced Placement
BA	break-an-argument
CAE	Council for Aid to Education
CBEST	California Basic Educational Skills Test
CLA	Collegiate Learning Assessment
CLEP	College-Level Examination Program
MA	make-an-argument
MCP	minimally competent person
NAEP	National Assessment of Educational Progress
NCLB	No Child Left Behind
PT	performance task
SAT	SAT Reasoning Test, a college entrance exam

1. INTRODUCTION

While there is little doubt that improving undergraduate students' critical thinking is an important higher education goal (Ennis, 1993; Kuhn, 1999; Facione, 2007; Facione, Facione, and Giancarlo, 2000), only recently have higher education institutions started exploring standardized testing to evaluate their success at achieving that goal. The Council for Aid to Education (CAE) has addressed the growing interest in measurement of higher education outcomes with the development of a constructed-response test of critical thinking, the Collegiate Learning Assessment (CLA). The CLA, which consists of mini work samples, tests a combination of high-level cognitive skills, and emphasizes value-added in its reports. It is entering only its fifth year of test administration in colleges and universities; hence, it is a relatively new test. Given its newness, institutions are still grappling with how best to interpret CLA results and apply them to their unique institutional goals.

The approach that CAE promotes for interpretation of CLA scores is institution-level "value-added," in which the progress students are making at one school is compared to the progress made by students at other colleges. *Progress* on the CLA is measured by comparing the freshman mean at a school to the senior mean at that school after controlling for SAT or ACT score differences between the two groups. This value-added approach to score reporting is central to the CLA program (Klein, 2007; Klein, Shavelson, Benjamin, and Bolus, 2007; Klein, Freedman, Shavelson, and Bolus, 2008).

Although value-added is CAE's approach, it is not the only possible approach to CLA score interpretation. Other, more traditional, approaches involve comparing a school's scores to that of other schools, or comparing a school's scores to some benchmark (or standard) for performance. The first approach, comparing one school's scores to that of other schools, can be conducted using information provided in the CLA reports to schools. Schools receive their freshman and senior mean scores and can compare them to all other schools included in the CLA report. Although the first approach to score interpretation can be conducted with data provided in the CLA reports, the latter approach to score interpretation—namely, comparison to a benchmark for performance—cannot be accomplished using CLA reports because no benchmarks or standards are provided by CAE. Instead, to answer the question, "Is a given CLA score considered 'satisfactory' or not?" a school would need to conduct a standard-setting study to establish its own benchmarks for purposes of interpretation.

However, to do so, schools are faced with two challenges. First, they need access to CLA test materials. If schools could see the test content, questions, scoring rubric, and answers at various score levels, they could begin to answer the aforementioned question for themselves. Due to test security considerations, only one CLA test prompt has been publically released (see Appendix A); however, the release of this test prompt along with sample answers could begin to allow schools to create their own standards.

The second challenge schools face is using an appropriate methodology to establish their standards. Most school administrators are not familiar with standard-setting methodology or how to determine whether the resulting standards are reliable and accurate. Moreover, whereas many studies have examined standard-setting methodologies for multiple-choice measures, research on standard-setting methods for constructed-response measures is sparse; hence, there is little guidance on the success of standard-setting techniques for measures such as the CLA.

Therefore, the RAND Corporation, in cooperation with CAE, conducted a study to examine the feasibility of one promising approach for gathering and summarizing faculty views about what constitutes satisfactory performance on the CLA. One goal of this exercise was to assist schools and students in developing their own standards that meet their unique institutional values.[1] These "local" standards are intended to complement and supplement the value-added information the CLA already provides by establishing fixed (i.e., not just relative) benchmarks against which to measure progress.

We designed our standard-setting technique with issues of validity and reliability in mind. In our technique, panels of four to five faculty members participate in a three-step process consisting of (1) setting standards individually, (2) arriving at consensus within their panel, and (3) participating individually in a validation sorting task (described below). The use of three steps allowed us to compare results from each step to evaluate the validity and reliability of the resulting standards. More specifically, we examined the following general research questions:

- Does the individual standard setting produce similar results across individuals? That is, when panel members individually (i.e., before consulting with other panel members) set standards for the range of performance that is considered adequate, proficient, or exemplary, are those standards similar to those of other panel members?

---

[1] Institutions vary in their expectations for performance; hence a "one-size-fits-all" approach (such as the use of national standards for performance) is not applicable. Consequently, the results in this study are for demonstration purpose only, and should not be interpreted as national standards for performance on the CLA. Instead, schools should establish their own standards that reflect their unique institutional goals and values.

- Does the consensus step produce results that are similar to the individual step? That is, when panel members discuss their individual standards with other panel members and produce a set of standards agreed upon by the group, are those standards similar to the individual standard-setting results?
- Does the consensus step produce similar results across panels? That is, when two separate panels are convened using the same procedures, are the standards similar?
- Does the sorting step indicate that panelists could apply their group consensus standards to a new batch of answers? That is, when panel members are blind to the scores of responses, can they validate their standards by correctly sorting a set of randomly ordered responses into the different performance standards?
- Are panel members confident in the standards they set?

The next portion of this report describes the CLA constructed-response tasks and measurement approach. We then discuss existing standard-setting methods and the method we developed for use with the CLA and tests like it.

THE COLLEGIATE LEARNING ASSESSMENT

The CLA differs from other tests in several ways, including its test format, its emphasis on measuring performance, and its emphasis on school-level value-added reporting. For example, the CLA is an entirely constructed-response measure; there are no multiple–choice items on the test. One advantage of constructed-response measures over multiple-choice tests is that an open-ended response mode has the potential for greater fidelity between test demands and performance demands in real-world settings, and fidelity is a key design feature of the CLA (Hersh, 2006). As noted by Norris (1989), "simply possessing critical thinking abilities is not an adequate educational attainment—the abilities must be used appropriately" (p. 22). This same philosophy has led CAE to incorporate a variety of constructed-response tasks and task formats into the CLA test design. The CLA includes multiple make-an-argument tasks (MAs) and break-an-argument tasks (BAs), as well as an assortment of performance tasks (PTs). Because the CLA response format emphasizes performance in simulated real-world settings, it is not intended to measure a single unidimensional construct. Instead, the CLA measures several interdependent constructs that together contribute to performance in real-life settings. More specifically, the CLA requires students to apply several aspects of critical thinking, including problem solving, analytic reasoning, and written communication skills, in explaining the basis for their answers. The PTs in particular are essentially mini samples of performance in real-world critical thinking contexts.

The performance assessed on the CLA is consistent with, although not limited to, the types of behaviors described in various definitions of critical thinking. For example, the aspects of performance evaluated in scoring the PTs and essay tests are very similar to Ennis's (1993) definition of critical thinking performance. In his definition, Ennis describes the following set of interdependent behaviors: judging the credibility of sources; judging the quality of an argument, including the acceptability of its reasons, assumptions, and evidence; identifying conclusions, reasons, and assumptions; developing and defending a position on an issue; asking appropriate clarifying questions; planning experiments and judging experimental designs; defining terms in a way appropriate for the context; being open-minded; trying to be well informed; and drawing conclusions when warranted, but with caution. The CLA's PT, MA, and BA tasks are designed to require students to demonstrate their skill at performing exactly these types of behaviors. For example, on PTs, students must provide a reasonable solution to a problem, justify that solution with their critical assessment and analysis of the test materials, and then effectively communicate their decision and reasoning in writing. Therefore, as mentioned previously, CLA performance is also dependent on what some would call problem solving, analytic reasoning, and written communication skills.

As mentioned previously, another defining feature of the CLA is its emphasis on value-added measurement. In essence, CLA results are presented as improvement relative to other schools, i.e., whether improvement is more, less, or about the same as improvement at other institutions. In each participating institution, performance of exiting seniors is compared to the performance of entering freshmen after controlling for SAT score differences. This value-added approach allows schools to compare the level of value-added at their school to value-added at other schools. Doing so directs attention away from trying to meet a single performance standard and toward amount of improvement regardless of the ability or skill level of entering students (Klein, 2007; Klein, et al., 2007).

CLA Tasks Types

The CLA consists of three types of constructed-response tasks: MAs, BAs and PTs. The CLA MA tasks are analytic essay writing tasks. The MA prompts are short, consisting of a one- or two-sentence statement or opinion about an issue. Students are asked to either agree or disagree with the statement and support their answers with evidence from history, knowledge from their coursework, current events, personal experiences, etc. The following is a sample MA prompt:

Government funding would be better spent on preventing crime than in dealing with criminals after the fact.

Students have 45 minutes to respond to the prompt. Responses are scored using a series of holistic criteria representing several aspects of critical thinking and writing.

The CLA BA tasks focus on critiquing someone else's argument. Students are presented with a short passage that is similar in format and content to common magazine articles, newspaper articles, and television news reports. The argument presented in the passage is designed to include several logical flaws or weaknesses. Students are instructed to critically evaluate the arguments presented in the passage, identify all flaws, and provide a rationale explaining why a particular statement is flawed. The following is a sample BA prompt:

The number of marriages that end in separation or divorce is growing steadily. A disproportional number of them are from June weddings. Because June weddings are so culturally desirable, they are often preceded by long engagements as the couples wait until the summer months. The number of divorces increases with each passing year, and the latest statistics indicate that more than 1 out of 3 marriages will end in divorce. With the deck stacked against "forever more" it is best to take every step possible from joining the pool of divorcees. Therefore, it is sage advice to young couples to shorten their engagements and choose a month other than June for a wedding.

Students have 30 minutes to critique the argument presented in the BA task. Responses are scored using a series of analytic items covering all reasonable flaws that could be identified in the passage and holistic items for overall writing and critical thinking.

The CLA PTs are designed to present realistic but fictional scenarios that require students to apply critical thinking, problem-solving, analytic reasoning, and writing skills. The PTs present the students with a number of documents (ranging from around five to ten) and a story line about the purpose of the task. The students are then asked to read the documents and respond to several (ranging from approximately three to seven) questions. Documents vary from task to task but can include tables and figures, technical reports, scientific journal abstracts of research findings, descriptions of key issues or terms, letters from concerned citizens, news editorial articles, transcripts from interviews, maps, etc. Questions also vary from task to task, but they generally require students to synthesize information across documents, evaluate the relative strengths and weaknesses of information presented in the documents, judge potential bias and credibility of sources, and come to a logical conclusion based on all of the information provided. A sample PT titled "Crime" is provided in Appendix A. Students have 90 minutes to read the materials and respond to the questions in the PT.

Scoring rubrics for the PTs differ and are tailored to the unique characteristics of each PT. However, all scoring rubrics include a combination of analytic and holistic scoring criteria. Although there are many types of analytic items on the scoring rubrics, the most common are items listing information that the students could raise in support of their argument, which receive one point if mentioned, and zero points if not mentioned. These cover the relevant information presented in the PT documents, as well as information that can be deduced or induced by comparing information across documents. The analytic items are generally given a score of 0 if students did not use the information in their response or 1 if they did. The number of analytic items varies, although typically there are over 20 analytic items for a given PT.

Holistic items are generally scored on 4- or 5-point scales. Multiple holistic items per PT require graders to provide holistic evaluations of different aspects of critical thinking, reasoning, and writing in the students' responses. These holistic items cover such areas as overall critical thinking and writing, as well as specific components of critical thinking, such as the students' use of the most relevant information in the PT and their recognition of strengths and weaknesses of information. Most PT scoring rubrics have around seven or eight holistic items. Although the method for computing a PT raw score is sometimes more complex, it is essentially a sum of every analytic item and every holistic item.

Because each PT scoring rubric is different, the raw score means and ranges also differ. PT scores are therefore rescaled such that each PT scale score distribution has the same mean and standard deviation (SD) as the SAT score distribution of the students taking that PT.[2] Only scale scores are reported to schools.

_____

[2] Though typically each subtest of the SAT has a mean of 500, a standard deviation of 100 and a cap of 800 points, the rescaling process for the PTs does not result in a PT mean of 500, standard deviation of 100 and cap of 800 points, for several reasons: (a) The SAT scores used to rescale the PTs are the *total* SAT scores (verbal plus math scores), not the individual subscale scores. (b) Because students participating in the CLA are already college students, they represent a range-restricted sample relative to the population of SAT test takers (which includes those who are not admitted to or opt not to attend college). To illustrate, the average freshman SAT score of students participating in the CLA in fall 2005 was 1248 with a standard deviation of 132. The PT scaling uses the mean and SD of the students who have take that PT, and that mean is noticeably higher than

Scoring for MAs, BAs and PTs is currently conducted by trained graders.[3] There are typically four to seven graders for each task. Training takes place over one to two days and includes an orientation to the task and the scoring rubric, followed by repeated practice grading a wide range of sample student responses. After training, graders complete a reliability check during which all graders score the same set of 25 student answers. Scorers with poor inter-rater agreement (determined by comparisons of raw score means and standard deviations across graders) or low inter-rater consistency (determined by correlations among the graders) are either further coached, or removed from scoring. Average inter-rater correlations for the PTs generally range from $r = .76$ to $.87$. Operationally, 10 percent of the PT responses are double-scored to estimate inter-rater reliability. The remaining 90 percent are single-scored.

ORGANIZATION OF THIS REPORT

The remainder of this report summarizes common standard-setting methodologies and presents the results of one method applied to the CLA. More specifically, Chapter 2 provides an overview of several standard-setting methodologies and guidelines for evaluating standard-setting methods, Chapter 3 discusses the standard-setting methodology used in the present investigation, Chapter 4 contains the results of the standard-setting study, and Chapter 5 presents conclusions based on those results. A summary evaluation of our standard-setting method, including suggestions for revisions to the method and some notes of caution regarding the use of standards resulting from this standard-setting methodology, is located in Chapter 6.

---

the mean of all students taking the SAT. (c) The rescaling process only ensures that the means and SDs of the PTs are equivalent to that of the SAT scores of the students taking them. It does not require that the same cap be placed on the PT distribution. As a result, although the standard deviation may be equivalent, the range of scores need not be. As of fall 2007, no cap is being placed on the PT scale scores and therefore scores exceeding 1600 are now possible.

[3] MAs and BAs will be machine-scored in fall 2008.

2. BACKGROUND ON STANDARD SETTING

Standard setting is the process by which cut scores are established to classify scores on a test into different categories or standards for performance. Cut scores (or cut points) are the points at and above which a test score is considered to qualify as meeting a performance standard and below which it does not. Examples of standards for performance include *passing* and *failing; expert, proficient, basic,* and *below basic*; and *unsatisfactory, satisfactory,* and *exceeds expectations.*

The reasons for establishing standards on a test are varied. One use of standards is for passing or failing people on professional licensing tests. Examples include state bar exams for licensing lawyers, statewide teacher certification tests, such as the California Basic Educational Skills Test (CBEST), and the Series 7 Licensing Exam for licensing of stockbrokers. Another use for standards is for classifying students into remedial classes or waiving basic course requirements. Examples include the College-Level Examination Program (CLEP) and Advanced Placement (AP) tests. Standards are also used for making school funding decisions, as in No Child Left Behind (NCLB), or for evaluating changes in nationwide or statewide performance over time as in the National Assessment of Educational Progress (NAEP). Still other uses for standards are decisions about whether or not to hire job applicants (i.e., pass/fail standards). One example is the Armed Services Vocational Aptitude Battery, which is used for selecting military personnel.

STANDARD-SETTING TECHNIQUES

There are numerous well-established techniques for setting standards (for reviews see Livingston and Zieky 1982; Berk, 1986; Hambleton, Jaeger, Plake, and Mills, 2000; Zieky, 2001; Cizek, Bunch, and Koons, 2004; Hambleton and Pitoniak, 2006; Zieky, Perie, and Livingston, 2006). Examples of several methods are summarized in Table 2.1. The earliest judgmental standard-setting methods include the modified Angoff method (1971), the Nedelsky method (1954) and the Ebel method (1972). The Angoff method focuses on establishing a cut point by estimating the probability that a minimally competent person (MCP) would get each item correct. The sum of the item probabilities is the location of the cut score. In the more complex Nedelsky method, judges identify multiple-choice options the MCP would eliminate as incorrect. Based on the remaining options, they estimate the probability that the MCP would get the item correct. The sum of the probabilities across all items on the test is the estimated cut point. Unlike the other two methods, Ebel's method involves estimating both the difficulty and importance of each test question in addition to estimating the probability that a MCP would get the items correct. The resulting cut score, therefore, takes into consideration the difficulty and importance of the items as well as the probability of getting them correct. Many variations on these and other methods have been developed and used in standard-setting studies and new variants continue to be explored (for reviews see Berk, 1986; Hambleton et al., 2000; Livingston and Zieky 1982; Zieky, 2001).

Table 2.1
Common Standard-Setting Techniques

Method	Author(s)	Process	Typical Test Type
Ebel	Ebel (1972)	Estimate the probability that MCPs would get each item correct. Estimate difficulty and importance of each item. Sum the probabilities across all items weighted by importance and difficulty to estimate cut point.	Multiple-Choice
Nedelsky	Nedelsky (1954)	Estimate probability that MCPs would get an item correct by identifying multiple-choice options they can eliminate as incorrect. The sum of the probabilities across all items on the test is the estimated cut point.	Multiple-Choice
Angoff	Angoff (1971)	Estimate the proportion of MCPs expected to answer each item correctly. Sum proportions across all items to produce cut score.	Multiple-Choice
Yes/No	Impara and Plake (1997)	Decide whether MCPs would get an item correct or not. Sum the yeses across items to produce cut score.	Multiple-Choice
Extended Angoff	Hambleton and Plake (1995)	Estimate the average score that MCPs would earn on each item. Sum estimates across all items to produce cut score.	Constructed-Response
Bookmark	Lewis et al. (1999)	Mark the point in a booklet of items arranged in order of difficulty at which MCPs would answer correctly all items occurring before that point.	Constructed-Response and Multiple-Choice

Body of Work	Kingston et al. (2001)	Examine each student's entire set of responses (multiple-choice and constructed-response) and sort the overall performance of each student into the various standards for performance.	Constructed-Response and Multiple-Choice
Integrated Judgment	Jaeger and Mills (2001)	Examine each student's entire set of responses (multiple-choice and constructed-response) and sort the overall performance of each student into the various standards for performance.	Constructed-Response and Multiple-Choice
Analytic Judgment	Plake and Hambleton (2001)	Sort student responses into the various performance standards, constructed-response and multiple-choice items considered separately.	Constructed-Response and Multiple-Choice
Contrasting Groups	Livingston and Zieky (1982)	People are separated into qualified and unqualified groups. Scores of the people in each group are used to determine the location of the cut scores.	Constructed-Response or Multiple-Choice
Borderline Group	Livingston and Zieky (1982)	People who are known to be MCPs are tested. Their median score is used as the cut score.	Constructed-Response or Multiple-Choice
Paper Selection	Loomis and Bourque (2001)	Identify responses that represent the performance of MCPs from a fixed set of definitively scored papers.	Constructed-Response

As a result of widespread use, there is a wealth of research on variations of the Angoff, Nedelsky, and Ebel methods. However, as noted in Table 2.1, these well-established methods are designed specifically for use with multiple-choice tests, not constructed-response measures (Plake and Hambleton, 2001; Hambleton and Pitoniak, 2006). Unfortunately, far fewer studies have explored methods for setting standards on constructed-response measures, and, as a result, there is no well-established technique for use with measures in the CLA.

Nevertheless, several methods for use with constructed-response measures have been proposed and tested in the recent literature.

One method is the *bookmark* method (Lewis, Mitzel, Green, and Patz, 1999). This method, which shares some features of an earlier technique developed by Klein (1986, 1991) for setting standards on constructed-response tests, was developed, in part, to accommodate tests with both multiple-choice and constructed-response formats and to reduce the high cognitive load placed on judges in the Angoff method (Mitzel, Lewis, Patz, and Green, 2001). Among the defining features of this method is the presentation of items to panel members in order of difficulty. Panel members place bookmarks at the points that separate those items that a MCP would get correct from those that they would not. Because items are ordered by difficulty, panel members are not required to estimate for every item the probability that a MCP would answer correctly (as in the other methods described above). Thus, the cognitive load for judges is reduced. Although the bookmark method is designed to accommodate constructed-response measures, its application to such measures is still relatively new; hence, more research on its efficacy is needed.

Another method used with both multiple-choice and constructed-response measures is the *body of work* method (Kingston, Kahl, Sweeney, and Bay, 2001). In this method, judges examine each student's entire set of responses (including multiple-choice items and constructed-response items) and classify (or sort) the overall performance of each student into the various standards for performance. Similar to the bookmark method, student responses can be ordered from low to high overall scores. Results of initial studies using this method suggest that the method is promising, but, like the bookmark method, it is new and additional research on its efficacy is still needed (Kingston et al., 2001).

A third method for use with constructed-response measures is the *analytic judgment method* (Plake and Hambleton, 2001). In this method, judges also sort student responses into the various performance standards, but—unlike the body of work method—student performance on each constructed-response and multiple-choice item is considered separately. Plake and Hambleton (2001) tested this method on three standard-setting panels; however, the results of those panels showed that judges must read a large number of student responses to achieve adequate levels of reliability. This need for large numbers of student responses may translate to considerable time commitments and high levels of demand on judges when using this method.

Although, as shown in Table 2.1, there are additional techniques for setting standards on constructed-response measures (see, for example, Loomis and Bourque, 2001; Faggen, 1994; Hambleton et al., 2000; Hambleton and Plake, 1995; Jaeger and Mills, 2001; Plake and Hambleton, 2001), the generalizability of these methods to the wide variety of constructed-response measures is still not well established (Hambleton et al., 2000). For this reason, no existing method is clearly the preferred method for use with all constructed-response measures.

EVALUATING STANDARD-SETTING METHODOLOGIES

As with any type of test interpretation, evidence of the reliability and validity of that interpretation is critical (AERA, APA, and NCME, 1999), and this is no less true for standards. Toward that end, specific features should be included in a standard-setting methodology to test whether the resulting standards are reliable and valid. However, the placement of a cut point for an educational or professional standard is always a decision involving judgment. Whether it is a good decision or a poor decision is determined in part by the processes used to arrive at it (Cizek, 2001).

Ultimately, the reason for establishing standards dictates certain features that should be included to ensure that the policy decisions resulting from those standards are appropriate.[4] In the case of this study, the reason for establishing standards is to accurately capture faculty expectations of what constitutes satisfactory performance on the CLA. Because an institution's view of what constitutes satisfactory versus unsatisfactory critical thinking performance in college is a policy judgment, this standard-setting endeavor is essentially a policy-capturing technique. Because policy judgments cannot be validated against some external objective criterion, there is no method that can produce a "true cut point;" rather, there are methods that can be applied to improve the decision-making process. Specifically, the validity of such standards is demonstrated by an examination of the process in which the policy judgment is captured.

Toward that end, several guidelines for evaluating and designing standard-setting study procedures have been proposed (e.g. Berk, 1986; AERA, APA, NCME, 1999; Hambleton, 2001; Kane, 2001), and following such guidelines is key to building a validity argument to demonstrate that the standard-setting results can be interpreted meaningfully. The following is a summary of those guidelines and a discussion of how each relates to our study described in Chapters 3, 4 and 5:

---

[4] Schools' purposes for establishing standards on the CLA could vary; however the goal of the standard-setting method described here is to aid interpretation of scale scores only. If a school wishes to set standards for high-stakes decisions, such as admissions or credentialing, it would require modifications to the methods to ensure that the standards are designed to address their intended use.

- Is the method appropriate for the particular educational assessment?

Because the most appropriate standard-setting method ultimately depends on the purpose and content of the test (Cizek, 1996; Livingston and Zieky, 1982), we considered a variety of factors in deciding which method is most applicable to the CLA, such as the use of constructed-response measures, and ultimately developed a method similar to the body-of-work method.

For example, one important consideration was the level of cognitive-load and time commitment that would be required of our panel members. Constructed-response measures can vary greatly in typical response length, content, and complexity. Some measures (e.g., NAEP) use multiple short-answer questions—each of which have a small possible range of scores, from 0 to 1 or 0 to 2— that are expected to be answered in a matter of minutes. Other measures include larger score ranges and longer responses; for example, the writing section of the SAT includes a single essay with an holistic score range of 1 to 6 and the expected student response time is 45 minutes. In addition, on measures using analytic scoring, there are typically a very narrow set of correct responses, while on holistically scored measures (such as the writing section of the SAT) there are potentially an infinite number of high-scoring responses.

Because constructed-response measures can vary greatly in typical response length, content, and complexity, such differing characteristics can present challenges for setting standards that can be unique to a particular measure. For example, the longer and more complex the student responses, the greater the time demand placed on the standard-setting panels for a given response. Relative to some constructed-response measures (such as short-answer items on NAEP), the responses on the CLA are long and complex, and the range of possible scores is large. As such, the amount of time required for panel members to read and cognitively process a large number of randomly ordered responses (as required in the analytic judgment method) would be prohibitive. In contrast, the ordering of responses, as in the bookmark method or the body-of-work method, has the potential to reduce cognitive load and time commitment. Consequently, the ordering of responses was a defining feature of the standard-setting method we developed for the CLA.

Our method is also designed to specifically address the CLA's use as a measure of institutional value-added. Because the very purpose of the CLA is to evaluate value-added by institutions, a fundamental assumption underlying this measure is that educators expect higher performance from exiting college seniors than from entering freshmen. We decided to test this assumption by asking faculty to set separate standards for freshmen and seniors as part of the standard-setting process.

A full description of the materials and procedures of our method is presented in Chapter 3.

- Is the purpose of the standards clearly specified and does the method address that purpose?

The purpose of these standards is to identify which scores on the CLA are considered unsatisfactory, adequate, proficient, and exemplary at a given school for use in examining how well the school is doing at meeting its own standards. Several features of the method are tailored specifically for this purpose. For example, some standard-setting methods provide faculty with information on how well students are performing on the measures. However, if faculty are aware of how students are doing on the measure, it might encourage them to raise or lower standards accordingly. Having faculty adjust their opinions based on such data may be desirable in certain contexts, such as setting cut points for employee selection tests. In our context, however, it is not desirable. Specifically, our goal is to assess faculty expectations independent of student performance so that a school can then evaluate its performance against those expectations.

As another example, our standards are not intended for use in selection decisions. Therefore, we did not compare the cut points to success or failure in some other domain. If we were interested in using the standards for selecting corporate executives, we would make different decisions in certain aspects of the process. We would select executives or experts from the company that would be using the test to serve on our panel, not university faculty, and we would collect data on how successful executives perform on the measure to validate the standards. Similarly, if a measure were to be used for making college admissions decisions, we would make modifications to the method to address that selection purpose. Therefore, depending on the purpose of the standards, the methodologies and resulting standards could be quite different from those described here.

- Are the panel participants representative of the relevant stakeholder groups?

Our panel was selected to include faculty from diverse disciplines and diverse schools. We selected our panel members for purposes of testing the methodology, not with the intention of making the panel representative of a particular group of stakeholders. Note that the panel used in our study reflects much more diversity than a single school does, and therefore our results are not representative of faculty perspectives at a single school. For a school creating its own standards, ensuring that a panel adequately represents the diversity of its own faculty is critical.

Information on the demographics of our panel is presented in Chapter 3.

- Are there multiple panels or other checks to examine the consistency, reliability, validity, and generalizability of the standards, and do the results of those checks support the validity of the standards?

Our study was conducted in two different locations on two separate sets of participants to examine whether the results could be replicated. In addition, we split participants into subgroups to compare results across different CLA PTs. This allowed us to examine whether the results are replicated across independent panels (i.e., by comparing results for both locations) as well as to generalize from one PT to another PT.

We also used a three-step process consisting of (1) setting standards individually, (2) arriving at consensus within a panel of four to five participants, and (3) participating individually in a validation sorting task where panel members (blind to the scores of responses) sort a randomly ordered set of responses into the different performance standards. Although the group consensus process is the step that is intended to yield the final standards, the other steps can lend support to the validity of the group standard-setting results. We collected results from each of the three steps, which permitted an empirical check of whether each step in the process was working as intended. That is, if any of the three steps produces drastically different standards, it would raise significant doubts about the validity of the standards. Finding similar results across the three steps lends additional credence that the standards are valid.

Chapter 4 presents the results of the research questions (outlined in Chapter 1) concerning the comparisons of results across locations, PTs, and the three steps to address the reliability, validity and generalizability of the standards.

- Did participants provide an evaluation of the standard-setting process, and was their evaluation supportive?

In our method, participants fill out a feedback form after completing the individual standard-setting process and the group standard-setting process. This feedback form asked participants to rate their confidence in the standards they set and was used to examine whether participants viewed the resulting standards as credible.

One of the research questions in the results chapter specifically addresses panel members' confidence in the results.

- Were panelists provided clear instructions throughout the standard-setting process, sample test materials (e.g., prompts, test items, scoring rubrics, sample responses)?

In our method, panelists were provided with CLA test prompts, scoring rubrics, student responses, and clear instructions throughout the process. The materials and instructions are documented in the standard study method in Chapter 3.

- Is the method documented in full from start to finish?

This report documents all aspects of the standard-setting method and results. Our documentation serves the dual purpose of providing evidence of the procedural validity of this method and an example for how to document the process should schools wish to replicate the method.

- Has the method been field tested and revised accordingly?

This entire study is intended as a field test of the method. Our test of the method did yield several suggestions for revisions to the method, which are summarized in Chapter 5. Future users of this method should also conduct a small field test (for example, using one PT and two groups of four or five faculty) in their own settings, to identify issues that are unique to their settings and to pilot the revisions we suggested based on our results before conducting the full standard-setting study. In addition, as discussed further in Chapter 6, this study only tested the method on CLA PTs. Therefore, for setting standards on CLA MAs and BAs, an additional pilot would be advisable.

3. STANDARD-SETTING STUDY METHOD

As discussed in the previous chapter, the use of multiple PTs, multiple panels, and the sorting step at the end, is part of building a validity argument to show that the results can be interpreted meaningfully. We used a three-step process consisting of (1) setting standards individually, (2) arriving at consensus within a panel of four to five participants, and (3) participating individually in a sorting task where panel members (blind to the scores of responses) sort a random set of set responses into the different performance standards. The first two steps of the method are similar to the first two steps of the body of work method and permit the comparison of the individual results to that of the results obtained by the group. In the first two steps, faculty receive the ordered responses and therefore know the scores of the student responses. Therefore, we added the third step in our method, the validation sorting task, to permit us to examine whether faculty could replicate their classification of responses into standards when they were blind to the scores of the responses.

The three-step process allowed us to conduct a planned empirical check on our standard-setting results by comparing the results across individuals, panels, and PTs, as well as across the three steps of the standard-setting process (see the general research questions presented at the beginning of Chapter 1).

PARTICIPANTS

We invited 27 college and university[5] administrators to nominate faculty from a diverse set of disciplines and tenures to serve as subject-matter experts on our standard-setting panels. The 27 colleges invited to participate were selected from the pool of colleges that were currently participating in the CLA. The schools were chosen to include small, large, public, and private institutions across the nation. The invited colleges each nominated several faculty to participate. We selected a sample of 41 faculty from the list of 90 nominated faculty. Participants were selected to ensure representation across a variety of disciplines, tenures, and genders. The colleges, nominees, and participants are therefore not a random sample of faculty within or across colleges in the United States. Demographic characteristics of the participants and their corresponding schools are displayed in Table 3.1.

---

[5] In the remainder of the report, we use the terms "college," "school," or "institution" interchangeably to refer to colleges and universities.

Table 3.1
Demographics of Panel Members and Their Colleges/Universities

Characteristics	Santa Monica Panel		New York Panel		All Panel Participants	
	n	Percent	*n*	Percent	*n*	Percent
Overall	18	44%	23	56%	41	100%
Panel member characteristics						
Instructor teaches at						
Public school	11	61%	6	26%	17	42%
Private school	5	28%	17	74%	22	54%
Number of students at instructor's school						
<3,000	4	22%	12	52%	16	39%
3,000 to 9,000	1	6%	2	9%	3	7%
>10,000	11	61%	9	39%	20	49%
Carnegie classification						
Baccalaureate	4	22%	9	39%	13	32%
Master's	4	22%	5	22%	9	22%
Ph.D.-granting	8	44%	9	39%	17	42%
Instructor's years of experience						
<5	0	0%	4	17%	4	10%
5 to 10	3	17%	1	4%	4	10%
>10	13	72%	18	78%	31	76%
Instructor teaches graduate courses						
Yes	9	50%	12	52%	21	51%
No	7	39%	11	48%	18	44%
Type of undergraduate course instructor teaches						
English	3	17%	5	22%	8	20%
History	-	0%	2	9%	2	5%
Philosophy	2	11%	2	9%	4	10%
Social sciences	4	22%	5	22%	9	22%
Math/statistics	1	6%	3	13%	4	10%
Physical/biological sciences	4	22%	3	13%	7	17%
Business/law	-	0%	1	4%	1	2%
Arts	1	6%	1	4%	2	5%
Other	1	6%	1	4%	2	5%

Note: Two participants in Santa Monica did not complete the demographics form. Therefore totals for Santa Monica on each demographic item are 16 and 89 percent for *n* and percent respectively.

MATERIALS

Student responses and corresponding scale scores from the CLA fall 2006 and spring 2007 testing cycles were used for this study. The current versions of the MA and BA prompts were not in operation prior to the start of this study; hence, there was not a sufficient bank of responses to use for setting standards on the MAs and BAs. Therefore, only PTs were used for demonstrating the standard-setting technique in this study. Regardless, the standard-setting technique described here would be applicable to MA and BA prompts as well.[6]

Because of the complexity of the scoring rubrics and the wide variety of correct (or incorrect) responses that students can construct, responses to the same PT with the same scale score often receive that scale score for entirely different reasons. As a result, responses with the same scale score often look very different. Consequently, someone tasked with judging the characteristics of a particular score level would need to read multiple responses at that level to form an overall impression of performance. In addition, with the use of many analytic items and several holistic items in scoring the PTs, the range of possible scale scores is large. Given the wide range in score points, reading a sample of responses at each scale score point would be an excessively time consuming and cognitively burdensome task for our standard-setting panels. Therefore, we opted to reduce the amount of score levels that panel members had to consider.

We did this by grouping responses into 11 scale score categories with each category representing a range of 90 scale score points (1 = 789 and lower; 2 = 790 to 879; 3 = 880 to 969; 4 = 970 to 1059; 5 = 1060 to 1149; 6 = 1150 to 1239; 7 = 1240 to 1329; 8 = 1330 to 1419; 9 = 1420 to 1509; 10 = 1510 to 1599; 11 = 1600 and up). We considered three primary factors in deciding the scale score categories. First, we hoped to reduce the cognitive load of the task (as discussed above). Second, we wanted to make sure that the variability of students would not be masked such that all students at a typical school would be likely to fall in one scale score category. The standard deviation for freshman or senior samples within a school is, on average, about 90 to 100 points. That is, at any one school, we would expect that no more than about 68 percent of freshmen, and possibly less, would score within 90 points of each other. Third, we wanted to ensure that rater error, which results in random

---

[6] Because students typically do not take all three types of CLA measures (i.e., MA, BA, and PT), and because the three tasks are designed to elicit different aspects of performance, we advise that schools set standards for each of the three types separately. Such separate standards would also provide greater diagnostic information to schools about areas of student strength or weakness.

scale score differences, did not produce essay groupings that appeared highly variable. The standard error of measurement for a response rated by one rater is about 60 to 70 points. Based on these three considerations, we opted to group the scale score categories into ranges of 90 points, which balanced maintaining a within-school diversity of categories against the standard error of measurement and the goal of keeping the number of categories manageable for the panel members. This 90-point grouping of scale scores is not the only option, and we acknowledge that grouping scale scores differently could result in different standard-setting results. This point is discussed further in Chapter 7.

Four responses (two senior and two freshmen) were randomly selected for inclusion in each of the 11 categories. Because the responses were randomly selected, scale scores varied across each category's 90-point scale score range. These student responses were arranged in a binder and grouped in the order of the 11 score categories. The lowest score category (scale scores of 789 and below) was located at the front of the binder, and the highest score category (scale scores of 1600 and above) was located at the end. The student responses within each section of the binder represented a random sample of responses in that score category. For an illustration of student responses, sample low-, mid- and high- level responses (i.e., scoring well below 900, between 900 and 1300 and well above 1300) for the Crime PT are located in Appendix B.

CAE provided us with a random sample of approximately 60 to 150 CLA student responses per task for use in this study. Because typically only 10 percent of the CLA responses are double-scored and that 10 percent is normally distributed over the scale scores, there was an insufficient number of double-scored responses at nearly every score range (in most score ranges there were none). We did submit a follow-up request for additional double-scored responses; however, due to complexities in how CAE stores and retrieves student responses, as well as the results of double scoring, the request could not be fulfilled in time for use in this study. Consequently, to obtain enough scored responses for use in the standard-setting materials and to maintain consistency in the reliability of scores in every category, the PT responses were single-scored only.

Feedback Forms

As a final component of the individual standard-setting process and the group consensus process, participants completed feedback forms. These forms asked participants to rate how confident they felt about the standards they set on a scale from 1 to 5 (where 1 = "not confident at all," 3 = "moderately confident," and 5 = "extremely confident"). The forms also asked yes/no questions such as: "Was it difficult to arrive at the standards?" and

"Do you think your perspectives on the standards will be different from those of other panel members?"

Questionnaire

At the conclusion of the last day just prior to panel adjournment, participants completed a questionnaire. The questionnaire was intended to measure the participants' overall impression of the PTs. The items were conceptually grouped to address the following general questions: Do participants think the test assesses an important educational construct? Do participants think this type of performance is being measured or taught in college courses? Do participants think the test measures what it is intended to measure (critical thinking skills, value-added, etc.)? Do participants think performance on the test would predict important life outcomes? Do participants think training people to do well on tasks like this will help people get ahead in life? How do participants think known groups would perform on this task?

This questionnaire is not intended as a comprehensive assessment of the construct validity of these PTs; however, it may provide some support for the content validity of the measure. These participants are not measurement experts, and, as such, their perceptions may reflect not content validity but rather face validity. Nevertheless, the participants can be considered subject-matter experts in the domain of higher education. Given their opportunity to closely examine the test prompts, score sheets, and the student responses, their answers to the questionnaire could, in some respects, reflect one form of expert judgment of the content validity of the measures. This questionnaire therefore may provide additional, but somewhat tenuous, evidence to support the content validity of these PTs.

Internal consistency statistics (coefficient alphas) for each set of items are shown in Appendix C. Sets of items for which coefficient alpha increased when the item was removed are noted in the appendix, and both the initial and improved coefficient alphas are presented.

PROCEDURE

Panel Assignments

Panels were split into two groups based on general region of the United States; 18 from the central and western half of the country participated in Santa Monica, and 23 from the central and eastern half of the country attended in New York. At each location, participants were placed into groups (or panels) of four to five participants. Group membership was predetermined such that every group had faculty from a variety of disciplines and a variety of tenures. Groups were then randomly assigned to set standards for one of five PTs (Brain Boost, Lake to River, Crime, Catfish, and Parks). Due to the smaller number of panel participants, Parks was not included in the Santa Monica panel.

Orientation to Performance Tasks

Hambleton (2001) suggests providing rater training to panel members before they begin individual standard setting. While we agree that comprehensive rater training would be ideal, it is not feasible for the CLA. Training of PT graders takes about two days, which would be prohibitive for a standard-setting panel. Instead, panel members were presented with the PT documents, test questions, and a scoring sheet (consisting of a three- to five-page description of the scoring points) used by the CLA graders. After reading through the PT and the scoring sheet, panel members discussed the information presented in the documents and the types of responses that students could provide based on that information. The first author of this report answered questions about the PT materials and the scoring sheets. This process lasted approximately one hour and was intended to orient the panel members to the PT on which they would be establishing standards.

Individual Standard Setting

Panel members first set standards individually. They were provided with the ordered binder of student responses for the PT to which they were assigned and asked to read the descriptions for the four performance standards for college freshmen and seniors (see Table 3.2).[7] They reviewed each response in each score category (in the ordered binder), and (as in the bookmark method) placed a bookmark at the category they felt represents the cut point for the beginning of each standard for performance (i.e., *Unsatisfactory/Unacceptable, Adequate/Barely Acceptable, Proficient/Clearly Acceptable,* or *Exemplary/Outstanding*). This process was completed simultaneously for entering freshman and exiting senior student performance. The purpose for setting freshman and senior standards simultaneously was twofold. First, because the CLA is designed as a measure of improvement from freshman to senior years, we wanted faculty to consider their expectations for the difference between senior and freshman performance on the measure when setting their standards. Second, our time with panel members was limited. Allowing faculty to consider both sets of standards

---

[7] The descriptors for each of the senior and freshman standards were created specifically for use with the CLA. CAE's Director of Research and Development collaborated with the authors of this report to establish the titles and descriptors for each standard.

simultaneously instead of requiring that they consider them separately was intended to reduce the amount of time required of panel members (i.e., separate consideration would have nearly doubled the amount of time required of panel members).

Panel members were also provided the following rules for setting the standards:

1. The standards should show how students should be expected to perform.
2. The standards should be realistic expectations for performance of college freshmen and seniors.

Panel members were not provided with information on the proportion of students receiving various scores. When standards are used for determining high-stakes educational consequences (e.g. certification, graduation tests, school accountability), it is common (although not necessarily desirable) for panel members to be provided information on the proportion of students at each score range. In such cases, panel members are asked to consider the consequences of their cut points. However, our goal for the standards is not determining high-stakes educational consequences, but rather determining faculty's expectations for performance at a given school regardless of how well the students are meeting those expectations. Faculty are very likely to adjust their standards (either lower or higher) if they knew the resulting proportions of students meeting them (which is why they are instructed to consider such information in other standard-setting situations). That adjustment would undermine our goal of determining faculty expectations regardless of how well the students are meeting those expectations. For this reason, we did not provide any information about the proportion of students at each of the score levels in the booklet.

Individual bookmark locations (i.e., cut points) for entering freshmen and exiting senior standards were recorded, and participants completed feedback forms individually before beginning the consensus process. The individual bookmark process took approximately three hours.

Table 3.2
Descriptors for the Freshman and Senior Standards for Performance on the CLA

College Freshman Standards for Performance
UNSATISFACTORY OR UNACCEPTABLE—Performance at this level is below or well below what is minimally acceptable for an entering college freshman.
ADEQUATE OR BARELY ACCEPTABLE—Performance at this level is minimally acceptable for an entering college freshman.
PROFICIENT OR CLEARLY ACCEPTABLE—Performance at this level represents what most entering college freshmen should be able to achieve.
EXEMPLARY OR OUTSTANDING—Performance at this level clearly exceeds what is expected from an entering college freshman.

College Senior Standards for Performance
UNSATISFACTORY OR UNACCEPTABLE—Performance at this level is below or well below what is minimally acceptable for a college graduate.
ADEQUATE OR BARELY ACCEPTABLE—Performance at this level is minimally acceptable for a college graduate.
PROFICIENT OR CLEARLY ACCEPTABLE—Performance at this level represents what most college graduates should be able to achieve.
EXEMPLARY OR OUTSTANDING—Performance at this level clearly exceeds what is expected from a college graduate.

Group Consensus

After completing the individual bookmark process, members of each panel (there was one panel per PT at each location) met to arrive at consensus regarding the cut points for the standards on that task. We instructed the panel members to use any process they would like for arriving at consensus.[8] The consensus process was completed for both entering freshman and exiting senior standards. Once consensus had been achieved, groups recorded the location of the cut points for each standard that was established by the group. Participants then completed feedback forms individually. The group consensus process took approximately an hour and a half.

---

[8] This freedom to choose the method of consensus may serve to reduce the standardization and agreement across panels; however, too many constraints on the process might alternatively be argued to produce results dictated by the method. Additionally, too many constraints on panel members could make them less likely to endorse the results.

Sorting

The last step in the standard-setting process was sorting a set of randomly ordered essays into the four standards. The purpose of this step was to determine whether participants could replicate the results of group consensus by sorting a set of randomly ordered responses into the four standards for performance (i.e., *Unsatisfactory/Unacceptable, Adequate/Barely Acceptable, Proficient/Clearly Acceptable,* or *Exemplary/Outstanding*). Participants were presented with approximately 11 freshman and 11 senior responses at varying score levels. Responses were selected to be a uniform distribution across the possible score range. Participants were blind to the scores of those responses. They were given two sets of responses, one for freshmen and one for seniors. That is, for one set, they were asked to group them by whether they were *Unsatisfactory/Unacceptable, Adequate/Barely Acceptable, Proficient/Clearly Acceptable,* or *Exemplary/Outstanding* for freshmen, and they were asked to group the second set of answers by whether they were *Unsatisfactory/Unacceptable, Adequate/Barely Acceptable, Proficient/Clearly Acceptable,* or *Exemplary/Outstanding* for seniors. However, participants were given both sets of responses (freshman and senior) at the same time (the freshman set was in one packet and the senior set was in another packet) and participants were left to decide which set to do first (freshman or senior) and whether or not to go back and forth between the two groups and make adjustments to either one (i.e., no specific instruction was given about this). The sorting process took about an hour for most participants. After finishing the sorting, participants completed the anonymous questionnaire and demographic forms.

4. STANDARD-SETTING STUDY RESULTS

In this portion of our report, we investigate several questions, and we present results for each separately. Because some questions addressed comparisons of PTs, while others addressed comparisons of locations, and still others addressed comparisons of the individual results to the group results, the data are summarized differently to satisfy each question. For example, if location and PT differences were not the focus of the question, the results were combined across PTs and across locations. For cases where locations or PT differences were the focus of the question, the locations were treated separately and/or the PTs were treated separately. (Tables summarizing all results for the individual, group consensus, and sorting steps by location and by PT are located in Appendix D and Appendix E. Results for the feedback forms are located in Appendix F.) In examining the results, we addressed the following questions.[9]

WAS THERE CONSISTENCY ACROSS INDIVIDUALS IN WHERE THEY PLACED THE CUT POINTS?

To answer this question, we examined the variation among individuals on a team in where they placed their bookmarks for each cut point. The standard deviation of the values for each cut point provides an index of this variation. Table 4.1 shows the standard deviations among panelists at each of the three cut points.

---

[9] In all tables and results (except where otherwise noted) the cut points reported are the bottom boundary of the band for that standard. For example, a *Proficient/Clearly* Acceptable cut point of 1310 and *Exemplary/Outstanding* cut point of 1480 indicates that scores of 1310 through 1479 fall within the *Proficient/Clearly* Acceptable band, and scores of 1480 and higher fall within the *Exemplary/Outstanding* band. The *Unsatisfactory/Unacceptable* category band includes all scores below the cut point for *Adequate/Barely Acceptable* and is not shown in the tables where lower bound cut points are presented.

Table 4.1
Standard Deviation in Cut Scores Across All Individuals and All Tasks

	Adequate/Barely Acceptable	Proficient/Clearly Acceptable	Exemplary/ Outstanding
	SD	SD	SD
Freshman	95	113	131
Senior	98	96	72

Because the location of the standards impacts how student performance is interpreted, a difference in opinion among panel members of 100 points or more could have a big impact on the evaluation of performance in some schools.[10] For example, for a school whose student performance has a standard deviation of 100 points on the PT, a 100-point increase in the cut point could result in as much as an additional 38 percent of students failing to meet the standard if the cut point is near the average PT performance at the school. If the cut point is far from the school's average scale score, the proportion of students who are affected by a 100-point change in the cut point would be much smaller.

Variation among individuals is to be expected, and we are less concerned about large variation between individuals if there is a small variation between panels in the group consensus results. However variation between individuals does indicate that the panel members' views are quite diverse. For a school evaluating its own standard-setting results, a standard deviation of 100 points would reflect disagreement among faculty such that some faculty (particularly those who were not involved in the standard-setting process) may feel that establishing a single standard to represent such divergent views is inappropriate.

WAS THERE GENERALLY MORE OR LESS AGREEMENT ACROSS INDIVIDUALS ON ONE OF THE THREE CUT POINTS THAN ON THE OTHER TWO?

To answer this question, we again examined the standard deviations across panelists for each cut point. A larger standard deviation indicates less agreement among individuals.

---

[10] The standard deviation for freshmen or senior samples within a school is, on average, about 90 to 100 points.

Table 4.1 shows a much larger standard deviation (indicating less agreement) for the freshman *Exemplary/Outstanding* cut point than for the freshman *Adequate/Barely Acceptable* cut point. In contrast, there was noticeably greater agreement for the senior *Exemplary/Outstanding* cut point relative to the senior *Adequate/Barely Acceptable* cut point. The fact that the results are reversed for freshman and senior cut points indicates that there is no consistent pattern of greater or lesser agreement for a particular cut point. The lack of consistent pattern is reinforced when we examine the results of Table 4.2, which shows no consistent pattern of greater variance across PTs on one cut point relative to another.

WAS THERE MORE AGREEMENT BETWEEN INDIVIDUALS ON SOME PTs THAN ON OTHERS?

We addressed this question by comparing the standard deviations of the cut points across the PTs, as shown in Table 4.2. The standard deviations do vary across PTs; however, the differences do not appear to be consistently higher or lower across the cut points. For example, relative to the other PTs, Brain Boost has the lowest standard deviation for the freshman *Adequate/Barely Acceptable* cut point, but the highest standard deviation for the freshman *Exemplary/Outstanding* cut point. The level of agreement therefore does not appear to be systematically higher or lower across the different PTs.

Table 4.2
Comparison of Standard Deviations for Individual Cut Points on Each PT

PT	Adequate/Barely Acceptable		Proficient/Clearly Acceptable		Exemplary/ Outstanding	
	Fresh.	Sr.	Fresh.	Sr.	Fresh.	Sr.
Brain Boost (n=9)	45	64	96	75	174	89
Crime (n=9)	79	64	84	47	45	40
Catfish (n=9)	64	110	110	119	119	75
Lake to River (n=9)	111	110	101	75	79	45
Parks (NY only, n=5)	75	99	75	117	161	104

DID THE CONSENSUS STEP TEND TO RAISE OR LOWER STANDARDS?

To examine this question, we compared the average cut points for the individual standard-setting step with the average cut points at the conclusion of the consensus step (i.e., we averaged the consensus results for each of the nine panels). Table 4.3 shows that the group averages are higher than the individual averages in every instance. The amount of increase, shown by the columns labeled "Difference," was moderate in some cases.

Table 4.3

Comparison of Averages for the Individual and Group Cut Points

| | Adequate/Barely Acceptable | | | Proficient/Clearly Acceptable | | | Exemplary/Outstanding | | |
	Ind. Average	Grp. Average	Diff. (Grp. – Ind.)	Ind. Average	Grp. Average	Diff. (Grp. – Ind.)	Ind. Average	Grp. Average	Diff. (Grp. – Ind.)
Freshman	922	939	17	1130	1139	9	1356	1389	33
Senior	1069	1097	28	1295	1328	33	1527	1563	36

DID THE CONSENSUS STEP INCREASE THE DIFFERENCE BETWEEN FRESHMAN CUT POINTS AND SENIOR CUT POINTS ON THE SAME STANDARD?

To answer this question, we subtracted the average freshman cut point from the average senior cut point for each standard to determine the size of the senior-freshman difference for the individual standard-setting step and the group consensus step. These differences are shown in Table 4.4.

Table 4.4
Comparison of Senior/Freshman Difference for the Individual and Group Cut Points

	Adequate/Barely Acceptable			Proficient/Clearly Acceptable			Exemplary/ Outstanding		
			Grp. –			Grp. –			Grp. –
	Ind.	Grp.	Ind.	Ind.	Grp.	Ind.	Ind.	Grp.	Ind.
Fresh.	922	939		1130	1139		1356	1389	
Sr.	1069	1097		1295	1328		1527	1563	
Diff. (Sr. – Fresh.)	147	158	11	165	189	24	171	174	3

As shown in Table 4.4, the difference between the senior and freshman cut points was higher for the group consensus process than the individual process for all three cut points. This increase in the senior-freshman difference was 24 points for the *Proficient/Clearly Acceptable* cut point, and 11 and 3 points for the other two cut points.

DID THE CONSENSUS STEP BRING THE CUT POINTS CLOSER TOGETHER (REDUCE THE STANDARD DEVIATIONS)?

To answer this question, we compared the standard deviations from the individual standard-setting step and the group consensus step. Table 4.5 shows that the standard deviations for the group consensus step were smaller than the standard deviations for the individual standard-setting step. This indicates that the consensus step did bring the cut points closer together.

Table 4.5
Comparison of Standard Deviations for the Individual and Group Consensus Cut Points

	Adequate/Barely Acceptable		Proficient/ Clearly Acceptable		Exemplary/ Outstanding	
	Ind.	Grp.	Ind.	Grp.	Ind.	Grp.
Freshman	95	74	113	81	131	89
Senior	98	75	96	62	72	45

Note: Standard deviations for groups are based on the sample of 9 groups. Standard deviations for individuals are based on a sample of 41 individuals.

WAS THERE CONSISTENCY ACROSS TASKS ON THE AVERAGE CUT POINTS?

We addressed this question by examining the variation in mean cut points across PTs. Table 4.6 shows that the standard deviations range from as low as 37 to as high as 98. We would expect some variation across tasks just by chance, and we would also expect some differences in the standard deviations across the cut points by chance; however, these data suggest that there is less variability in the senior cut points than in the freshman cut points.

Table 4.6

Comparison of Average Group Consensus Cut Points Across PTs

PT	Freshman Cut Points			Senior Cut Points		
	Adequate/ Barely Acceptable	Proficient/ Clearly Acceptable	Exemplary/ Outstanding	Adequate/ Barely Acceptable	Proficient/ Clearly Acceptable	Exemplary/ Outstanding
	Mean	Mean	Mean	Mean	Mean	Mean
Brain Boost ($k=2$)	880	1060	1330	1100	1280	1600
Crime ($k=2$)	1060	1240	1470	1190	1370	1560
Catfish ($k=2$)	930	1200	1470	1110	1380	1560
Lake to River ($k=2$)	920	1100	1370	1010	1280	1510
Parks (NY only, $k=1$)	880	1060	1240	1060	1330	1600
Standard deviation of mean cut points across the 5 PTs	74	83	98	67	48	37

Note: k is the number of panels contributing to the within-PT average. A sample size of 5 PTs was used to compute the standard deviations.

WAS THERE CONSISTENCY ACROSS PANELS ON WHERE THEY PLACED THE CUT POINTS FOR A GIVEN TASK?

To address this question, we examined the difference between the two panels' cut points for each PT. As shown in Table 4.7, for most of the Brain Boost cut points, there was no difference between the two panels. For the remaining tasks, many if not all of the cut points differed, but not by more than 90 points. This 90-point difference translates to a standard deviation of 64 points across the two groups and a standard error of 45 points for the average of their cut points. For example, assuming a standard deviation of 64 points, the standard error for the average of their cut points is reduced to 37 points when using three panels, and 29 points when using five panels for the same PT. Therefore, to obtain stable cut scores, several panels should ideally be included both within and across PTs.

A comparison of the standard deviations of cut scores within PTs (which range from zero to 64 points, as noted above) with the standard deviations across PTs (which range from 37 to 98 points, as shown in Table 4.6) illustrates that, for some cut points, the variation observed within PTs is smaller than the variation observed across PTs. Although PT scale scores are calibrated to a common scale with similar means and standard deviations, these findings are an indication that scale scores or faculty perspectives may not be completely equivalent across tasks at all scale score levels.

Table 4.7

Difference in Scale Score Points Between the Two Panels' Cut Points on Each PT

PT	Freshman Cut Points			Senior Cut Points		
	Adequate/ Barely Acceptable	Proficient/ Clearly Acceptable	Exemplary/ Outstanding	Adequate/ Barely Acceptable	Proficient/ Clearly Acceptable	Exemplary/ Outstanding
Brain Boost (k=2)	0	0	0	90	90	0
Crime (k=2)	0	0	90	90	90	90
Catfish (k=2)	90	90	90	90	90	90
Lake to River (k=2)	90	90	90	90	90	0
Parks (NY only, k=1)	—	—	—	—	—	—

Note: k is the number of panels. Parks was only examined by one panel; therefore a difference could not be computed.

WAS THE DIFFERENCE BETWEEN FRESHMAN AND SENIOR GROUP CONSENSUS STANDARDS CONSISTENT ACROSS PTs?

We addressed this question by subtracting the average freshman cut point from the average senior cut point for each group consensus standard to determine the size of the senior-freshman difference on each PT. The senior-freshman differences by PT are shown in the last three columns of Table 4.8. Brain Boost and Parks have large senior-freshman differences relative to the other tasks. For example, for a school whose student performance has a standard deviation of 100 points on the PT, a 220-point increase from freshman to senior performance could be as high as going from the 14th percentile to the 86th percentile from freshman to senior years. If the freshman and senior cut points are both below the school's mean or both above the school's mean, the change in percentile from freshman to senior would be much smaller.

Table 4.8

Difference Between Senior and Freshman Cut Points for Each PT

PT	Freshman Group Consensus Cut Points			Senior Group Consensus Cut Points			Difference (Senior − Freshman)		
	Adeq./ Barely Accept.	Prof./ Clearly Accept.	Exemp./ Outstand.	Adeq./ Barely Accept.	Prof./ Clearly Accept.	Exemp./ Outstand.	Adeq./ Barely Accept.	Prof./ Clearly Accept.	Exemp./ Outstand.
Brain Boost (k=2)	880	1060	1330	1100	1280	1600	220	220	270
Crime (k=2)	1060	1240	1470	1190	1370	1560	130	130	90
Catfish (k=2)	930	1200	1470	1110	1380	1560	180	180	90
Lake to River (k=2)	920	1100	1370	1010	1280	1510	90	180	140
Parks (NY only, k=1)	880	1060	1240	1060	1330	1600	180	270	360

Note: k is the number of panels.

DID THE SORTING STEP INDICATE THE PANELISTS COULD APPLY THEIR GROUP CONSENSUS STANDARDS TO A NEW BATCH OF ANSWERS?

To answer this question, we compared the average score of the PT responses sorted into a given category during the sorting task with the range of scores established by the group consensus procedure for that category. If the panelists applied their group consensus standards in a consistent way during the sorting task, we would expect the sorting task mean to fall within the consensus standard range. As shown in Table 4.9, the averages of the sorted PT responses do fall between the group consensus standard ranges for every standard except senior *Exemplary/Outstanding*. As shown in Table 4.10, the PT responses were classified into the correct category (based on their scale score) for a majority of the PT responses, and the correct or nearest category for 92 percent of the freshman and 96 percent of the senior PT responses. Because each PT response could be assigned to any of the four standards, if panel members were assigning PT responses randomly to categories, each PT response would have a one in four (25 percent) chance of being assigned correctly by chance alone. Therefore the fact that over 50 percent of the PT responses were classified in the correct category suggests that panel members were sorting PT responses at better than chance levels. Moreover, the correlation between the standard to which the PT response was assigned and the scale score of the PT response was .77 for the freshman PT responses and .78 for the senior PT responses. This also suggests that raters were doing better than chance alone in their assignment of PT responses.

Table 4.9

Comparison of Sorting Averages with the Standards Set by the Consensus Process

	Freshman				Senior			
	Unsatisf./Unaccept.	Adeq./Barely Accept.	Prof./Clearly Accept.	Exemp./Outstand.	Unsatisf./Unaccept.	Adeq./Barely Accept.	Prof./Clearly Accept.	Exemp./Outstand.
Group consensus standard (range of performance set for each standard)	938 and below	939 to 1138	1139 to 1388	1389 and higher	1096 and below	1097 to 1327	1328 to 1562	1563 and higher
Sorted PT average scale score[a]	876	1065	1302	1421	866	1195	1410	1471

Note: Standard ranges are computed using the cut point from the group standard-setting process as the bottom of the range and one point below the cut point for the next standard as the top of the range. The *Unsatisfactory/Unacceptable* standard range is all scores below the cut point for the *Adequate/Barely Acceptable* standard.

[a] Sorted PT average scale scores are the average scores of the PT responses sorted into that category. They are not cut points.

Table 4.10
Accuracy of Sorting as Measured by Percent of PT Responses Classified into the
Correct Standard

	Freshman	Senior
Correctly classified	53%	54%
Classified one standard lower or higher	38%	42%
Classified two or more standards lower or higher	8%	4%

Note: The freshman column totals to 99% due to rounding error.

WERE PANEL MEMBERS CONFIDENT IN THE STANDARDS THEY SET?

To address this question, we examined ratings of confidence provided by panel members on the individual and group consensus feedback forms. The ratings were measured on a scale from 1 to 5 where 1 = "not confident at all," 3 = "moderately confident," and 5 = "extremely confident." As shown in Table 4.11, panel members were on average more than "moderately confident" (where moderately confident is the anchor for a 3 on the scale from 1 to 5) with the standards they set and with the standards set by their group (see Appendix F). The ratings of confidence were slightly higher for the group consensus process than for the individual process.

Table 4.11
Confidence Ratings Before and After the Group Standard-Setting Process

Questions About the Standard-Setting Process	Mean	SD
How confident do feel about the standards you set?[a]	3.44	.67
How confident do feel about the standards set by your group?[a]	3.83	.64

[a] Rated from 1 to 5 where 1 = "not confident at all," 3 = "moderately confident," and 5 = "extremely confident."

5. STANDARD-SETTING STUDY CONCLUSIONS

We addressed several questions in the previous chapter that illustrate the type of questions schools should ask to ensure that the standard-setting procedure is functioning as intended. These questions are not an exhaustive list of questions that could be posed and answered about the standard-setting process and results. Instead, they were selected to illustrate the types of question that could and should be examined as part of a standard-setting process.

The first question ("Was there consistency across individuals in where they placed the cut points?") provides an overall assessment of the amount of agreement among panel members. Among our panel members, the standard deviations were large. Given that our panel included faculty from a variety of universities, it is possible that within a given university, the standard deviations could be much smaller. Schools should examine the individual variation among their panel members.

The next two questions ("Was there generally more or less agreement across individuals on one of the three cut points than on the other two?" and "Was there more agreement between individuals on some PTs than on others?") are intended to examine whether the standard-setting perceptions vary systematically from task to task or cut point to cut point. Ideally, they should not. However if they do, it suggests the need for greater caution in interpreting the results of those cut points that have greater variance relative to others. In our data, there were no consistent differences in the variance of perceptions across PTs or across cut points.

The questions comparing the results of the consensus process to the results of the individual process (i.e., "Did the consensus step tend to raise or lower standards?" and "Did the consensus step increase the difference between freshman cut points and senior cut points on the same standard?") are included to confirm that the consensus process is working as intended. If the consensus discussion was dominated by someone who differs noticeably from the rest of the group, the resulting group cut points would be significantly higher or lower than the average of the panel's individual cut points. In our data, the consensus process produced small-to-moderate increases in the cut points relative to the individual process. This suggests that the consensus process may be more strongly influenced by those with stricter cut points (i.e., those who hold people to a higher scale score) relative to those with lenient cut points (i.e., those who hold people to a lower scale score). Studies do show that judgments are consistently more extreme after group discussion (Fitzpatrick, 1989). In the case of our study, perhaps our participants tended to hold the view that cut points should be strict, and after hearing that others were stricter, the group decisions reflected that tendency toward strictness. It is not clear whether changes as a result of group discussion should be considered problematic in standard-setting studies (Fitzpatrick, 1989). However, if our goal is to develop standards that participants endorse, it does seem reasonable to permit faculty to discuss their expectations with others before settling on final cut points, even if those final cut points change. This is particularly relevant for ensuring faculty confidence in the standards, considering that faculty were more confident in their groups' cut points than they were with their individual cut points. Although this increase in consensus cut scores relative to individual cut scores was not anticipated, it suggests that future applications of this method should collect additional information from panel participants (e.g., perceptions of their own leniency or strictness, accuracy, or credibility relative to others in the group and other faculty in general) before and after they complete the consensus process, to further investigate the causes of such score increases or decreases.

Another check to ensure that the consensus process is working as intended (i.e., individual panel members' views are contributing to the group consensus results) includes addressing the following question: "Did the consensus step bring the cut points closer together (reduce the standard deviations)?" If the consensus process is working as intended, there should be less variability across panel cut points than there was across individual cut points, as was the case in our data. If the standard deviations for the group cut points are higher than the individual cut points, then it is an indication that the consensus process is not producing reliable cut points. In our results, the consensus step did produce smaller standard deviations across panels relative to the individual standard-setting results.

We also included three questions ("Was there consistency across tasks on the average cut points?" "Was there consistency across panels on where they placed the cut points for a given task?" and "Was the difference between freshman and senior group consensus standards consistent across PTs?") to determine if cut points could be considered equivalent regardless of which task was used for setting standards. Our results showed that the standard deviations across tasks were in some cases somewhat large and in other cases not large at all. In addition, the standard deviation within tasks was smaller than the standard deviation between tasks for four of the six cut points. Essentially, for some cut points, there was greater variance across tasks than within tasks. This suggests either that faculty perspectives across tasks are not completely equivalent or that the tasks themselves are not completely equivalent at every score range. Because of this finding, and given that CLA scores are averaged across tasks and not provided separately by task, we suggest that the standard-setting process should, if possible, be conducted on multiple tasks and then the cut points should be averaged.[11] Given that CLA scores are not reported separately by PT, averaging the results would help to ensure that the overall cut points established by the standard-setting process will generalize to the broader set of CLA PTs on which CLA scores are based. Another suggestion would be to have the same panels evaluate multiple sets of PTs. After establishing cut points for each PT individually, the panels could then come to consensus on a single set of cut points that apply across the full set of PTs examined.

In the individual and group standard-setting steps, participants relied on a binder of responses ordered from low to high scores. Because the preordering of responses could bias participants into creating categories that they would not replicate under other conditions, we established a third step to test that possibility. In other words, the sorting step is intended to test whether faculty can apply the standards to a new set of responses when they are blind to the scores of the responses. If they cannot, it threatens the validity of the results produced using the ordered binder. We therefore asked whether the sorting step indicates that the panelists could apply their group consensus standards to a new batch of answers. Our results showed that the average score of the answers that were placed into a given standard did fall between the upper and lower bounds of that standard in all but the senior *Exemplary/Outstanding* Category. This shows that the panel members were (with one exception) able to classify PT responses in a manner that, overall, was consistent with the standards they set. However, individual PT responses were classified into the correct standard only about 50 percent of the time. While this is better than would be expected by chance, it is not at a level that would be considered highly accurate.

Three sources of unreliability could have contributed to the low percentage of correctly classified PT responses observed in our study. First, sorting occurred at the end of the day, after participants had spent several hours in the individual and consensus standard-setting processes. Therefore, it is possible that fatigue reduced sorting accuracy. In addition, many of our panel members completed the sorting step quickly relative to a few other panel members. It is possible that panel members rushed through the sorting step and did not dedicate adequate time to the judgment process. Second, it is also possible that our panel members are simply not highly reliable judges of performance on the CLA, regardless of

---

[11] If PT scale scores are not equivalent at all score ranges, the resulting standards when averaged will not be exact estimates of the standards for performance on any given PT. PT means and standard deviations are equated, but the underlying distributions are not equated; therefore, it is not known whether PT scale scores can be considered equivalent at *all* score ranges.

fatigue or time spent on task. Due to time constraints, we did not provide any formal training to the panel members on how to score these PT responses, nor did we make any attempt to calibrate their scoring. Such lack of training can result in low agreement across raters in grading constructed-response measures. Third, it is possible that the scale scores assigned by graders were not highly reliable. More specifically, the responses provided were only scored by one CLA grader. Given that a score from one CLA grader is less reliable than a score based on an average of two CLA graders, it is possible that unreliability in the single-scored PT responses could have contributed to the low classification accuracy that was observed in the sorting process. In addition to the possible causes of low reliability, we also only provided the panel members with 10 to 12 responses to sort. While this would not be expected to affect the proportion of correctly classified responses, it does affect the reliability of the mean estimates of the PT responses grouped in each standard. More specifically, as the number of PT responses goes up, the standard error of the mean estimate in each category will go down.

The finding that many PT responses were not correctly classified by our panel though correlations between the score-based category and panel members' judgments were high (.77 and .78) suggests that sorting results were not purely random. Therefore, changes to the sorting task directed at reducing sources of error variance in the sorting step could potentially improve the proportions of correctly classified responses. More specifically, the sorting step could be modified in four ways to attempt to reduce the error of the sorting PT response means. First, all PT responses used in a sorting task could be scored by at least two CAE graders and the average of the scores could be used to determine to which category the PT response belongs. This would serve to boost the reliability of the PT response scale scores. Second, the time dedicated to the sorting step could be extended. The standard-setting process could take place over at least two full days, with individual standard setting and consensus taking place on the first day, and the sorting step taking place on the second day. Our participants spent around one hour sorting 10 to 12 senior and 10 to 12 freshman PT responses. That translates to about 2.5 minutes per response. However, because we suspect that our panel may have rushed through the process, we instead suggest allowing panel members to dedicate up to 10 minutes per response during the sorting task. Therefore, we advise moving the sorting step to a second day and allowing more time for the process. Third, a much larger sample of PT responses should be used in sorting to ensure that sufficient numbers of responses are available at all score ranges. In our study, the number of sorted responses ranged from 10 to 12 and represented a uniform distribution of responses (i.e., they included responses from the entire score range), which were presented to participants in a random order. Increasing the number of responses that are sorted will permit more accurate estimates (i.e., reduce the standard error) of the sorting means. This reduction of the standard error will increase the accuracy of conclusions that the mean of the sorted responses do or do not fall within the bounds of the standards set during the consensus process. Lastly, we suggest that, as the number of PT responses to be sorted increases, so too should the amount of time dedicated to sorting. These suggested changes could allow the sorting step to serve as a useful check on whether the respondents can apply the consensus cut points to unscored responses.

It is worth noting that the number of panel members can also have an effect on the reliability of the estimates produced in the standard-setting process (Raymond and Reid, 2001). For example, Jaeger and Mills (2001) found that the standard error of average cut scores in their standard-setting studies (using the integrated judgment method) were a function of both the number of panel members and the number of student responses considered. Even though number of participants mattered, they reported diminishing returns beyond 15 to 20 participants. Though studies do examine the effects of the number of participants on cut-score reliability, Raymond and Reid (2001) reviewed studies on the appropriate number of panel members and conceded that the appropriate number of participants is not clearly established and varies both within and across different standard-setting methodologies. Therefore, they suggest that after a standard-setting study is conducted, the results should be used to inform the appropriate number of participants in similar applications of the method. In our study, we used a panel size of four to five members with a total of 41 participants overall. This size of panel worked well for our process. It included enough people to ensure that comparisons across panels could be made with some reliability, but it was not so large that the process of consensus would be burdensome by including too many viewpoints or would allow group members to remain silent and unnoticed during the process. Moreover, it balanced the panel size against the need for multiple panels, which is a key component of our standard study technique. Specifically, our number of individual participants (41) far exceeded Jaeger and Mills' recommendations, and the number of panels (9) permitted the examination of differences across PTs as well as within PTs. While the panel sizes in our technique could be increased (i.e., above four to five people per group) in an attempt to improve reliability within a panel, another alternative would be to include more panels (i.e., more than nine groups) to improve reliability of the group consensus results. For example, instead of including two panels (with four to five members) per PT, there could be four panels (with four to five members) per PT. This would essentially double the number of groups, making the group consensus results more reliable. Because the group consensus results are intended to be used for computing the final standards, our goal is to make the group findings as reliable as possible. Therefore, given the choice between increasing the number of participants within a panel or increasing the number of groups, we advise increasing the number of groups.

The last question we asked ("Were panel members confident in the standards they set?") was intended not only to confirm that the consensus process increases rather than decreases confidence in the standards but also to indicate whether the faculty will endorse the standards established during the standard-setting process. While it is unrealistic to expect that, on average, all panel members will feel extremely confident in the results of the standard-setting process, it is desirable for the panel members to feel at least moderately confident in the results. In our panel, the consensus process did increase confidence ratings relative to the individual standard-setting confidence ratings, and faculty were more than moderately confident about both the individual and consensus standards they set.

Lastly, as with any standard-setting study, the results are limited by certain aspects of the research design. One example of a limitation in the present investigation is the choice to group responses into eleven 90-point categories. As described previously, this decision was based on the desire to balance the number of score categories that panel members had to consider against keeping as much meaningful variability in scores as possible. However, other options such as using 70-, 80- or even 100-point categories would be just as reasonable, and it is likely that the standard-setting results would be somewhat sensitive to different sized categories. Another limitation concerns our decision to ask panel members to consider freshman and senior standards simultaneously. Doing so may have primed participants to assume that the standards for each should be very different, thus producing an artificially induced result. Perhaps if we had one panel set only freshman standards and a different panel set senior standards, the resulting senior-freshman difference between the standards would have been much smaller or much larger.

6. SUMMARY AND NOTES OF CAUTION

In this study, we demonstrated a technique for the CLA that can be used for establishing uniform standards within a college or even within a department that are tailored to the institution's goals and mission. Using the guidelines for evaluating a standard-setting study (as described in Chapter 2), our study was designed to build a validity argument that the results can be interpreted meaningfully. Specifically, the validity argument included the following:

- The standard-setting method was carefully selected to address the unique features of the CLA.

- The purpose of the standards was clearly specified and the method was designed to address that purpose.

- The panel participants were representative of stakeholders for our aim— namely, testing the method. Schools developing their own standards should ensure that their own stakeholders (i.e., faculty at their institution) are adequately represented in their panels.

- We used multiple panels, multiple PTs, and multiple methods (i.e., the three-step process) to test the consistency, generalizability, and validity of the standards. The results suggested that, with modifications to the process including using double-scored responses and increasing the number of responses used in the sorting task, the time for the sorting task, and the number of panels, the overall validity argument could be strengthened. Nevertheless, our results were supportive of the methodology.

- Participants indicated that they were confident in the standards they set, particularly those that were set by their group, suggesting that the resulting standards would be supported by the faculty.

- Panelists were provided clear instructions throughout the standard-setting process, PT test prompts and documents, detailed scoring rubrics, and sample student responses.

- The method was documented from start to finish.

- The method has now been field-tested for use with CLA PTs. Based on the findings of this field test, we identified several suggestions for improvements to the method (summarized in Chapter 5). Future users of this method should also conduct a small field test (for example, using one PT and two groups of four or five faculty) in their own settings to identify issues that are unique to their settings, and to pilot the revisions we suggested based on our results before conducting the full standard-setting study. In addition (as described in greater detail in the notes of caution below), this study tested the method only on CLA PTs. Therefore, for setting standards on CLA MAs and BAs, an additional pilot would be advisable.

On the whole, our findings suggest that with slight modifications (as described in Chapter 5) this is a promising method for setting standards on the CLA.

As mentioned previously, although there is some research on the application of traditional standard-setting methods to constructed-response measures and a growing list of new methods (see for example, Faggen, 1994; Hambleton et al., 2000; Plake and Hambleton, 2001), the generalizability of these methods to the wide variety of constructed-response measures is still not well established (Hambleton et al., 2000). Although we do acknowledge that the method presented here is not the only method, it was shown in this study to have promise for establishing standards on the CLA and could be applied to other constructed-response measures as well.

Overall, the development of standards at a school will provide a much clearer picture of performance on the CLA. However, we do offer several notes of caution in using the results of this study.

First, our panels were composed of faculty from a variety of colleges and universities—public and private, large and small, and those granting baccalaureates, master's degrees, and Ph.Ds. It is very likely that if faculty were to set standards for their own school or their own department, the resulting standards would differ from those presented here. Therefore, the perspectives of the faculty panels used in this study are unlikely to be representative of every school. For this reason, the cut points for the standards presented in this paper are for illustration of the method only and should not be applied to institutions. Instead, the method should be repeated using a representative sample of faculty from within a single institution only, and the results of that standard-setting process should be used for that school.

Second, we also note that the technique we demonstrated in this paper asks faculty members to set standards for students, not schools. Therefore, standards established using this technique are applicable only to students. More specifically, this technique does not determine what percentage of *Unsatisfactory/Unacceptable* or *Proficient/Clearly Acceptable* performance, is reasonable for a given school. Put another way, the establishment of standards is not intended to determine what proportion of a school's students *should* meet the standards, but only how many *do* meet the standards. The issue of what proportion *should* meet the standards is an entirely different policy question, one which this study does not address. Regardless, we do strongly caution against setting arbitrary expectations for percentages of student performance within schools. Instead, we suggest that schools use the individual-level standard-setting process we describe in this study to examine the current proportions of students at each level in their school and aim to improve them. Doing so focuses attention on improvement, the basic tenet of CAE.

Third, the CLA data samples of freshmen and seniors for each institution are not necessarily a representative random sample of freshman or senior students within a given school. If a school's sample is not representative, then it would be inappropriate to draw conclusions about whether or not the school's students in general are meeting their standards. Although schools are encouraged to select a random stratified sample of freshmen and seniors, each school selects and recruits the sample themselves. Recruiting practices vary from school to school such that participation at some schools is completely voluntary, at others rewarded with an incentive to participate, and at still others, required as part of a course. However, despite the differences in sampling practices at various colleges, the average SAT score of freshman and senior samples is on average very similar to the mean SAT score for freshmen and seniors at that university.[12] This suggests that, on average, senior and freshman samples at colleges are not unlike the senior and freshman populations at those schools, at least with respect to measured ability. Even so, it is possible that freshman and senior samples at a school are not representative of all students at that school. For this reason, colleges hoping to establish standards and then estimate the proportion of students performing at those standards must either ensure that they test a truly random (or stratified random sample), or test their entire freshman and senior classes.

Fourth, we suggest caution with respect to classifying individual student-level performance on the CLA. The CLA is a measure designed for use at the school level. When analysis is at the school level, individual student-level score reliability does not need to be high to achieve high reliability at the school level. For this reason, the CLA takes only one sample of performance from each student and assigns a score from only one grader. This means that individual student-level results are not as reliable as they could be if a student

---

[12] Note that because the CLA reports value-added results after controlling for differences in ACT/SAT scores, differences between the school's sample and its population are of less concern for drawing conclusions about value-added than they are about the proportion of students meeting a school's standards.

were to complete more than one assessment or if their response was assigned an average score over two graders. This also means that the standard error of measurement is not as low as it could be, nor as low as it should be if individual student-level scores have high-stakes consequences. The CLA has never been a high-stakes individual-level assessment tool.[13] However, if a school intends to judge an individual student against its standards, the issue of the reliability of a student's score becomes much more of a concern. Error due to unreliability in individual-level scores could result in some students being classified into the wrong standard of performance, particularly if their performance is near the cut point. For this reason, if an individual student (as opposed to groups of students) is going to be judged against standards, we strongly advise that the student complete several CLA tasks and that the student's response be double-scored.

Fifth, with respect to the use of standards for anything other than their intended purpose, we also advise caution. As mentioned previously, standards are often set to establish cut points at the individual level for credentialing, certification exams, qualifying for jobs, or even making policy decisions regarding the allocation of resources. The method for establishing standards described in this paper is not designed for such purposes, and we strongly caution against using CLA standards established using this technique in a manner that was not intended. To illustrate, for circumstances in which cut points on a test are used to qualify people for jobs, panel members setting such cut points should be given specific instruction regarding performance on the job and the meaning of a minimally competent person in that job. They would be directed to set only one cut point—namely, the point below which people do not have the qualifications necessary to perform the job. Lastly, in such an employment context, the effect of that cut point on race and gender groups would need to be examined in accordance with employment laws. The results of such a study might result in very different cut points for one job versus another job. Therefore, the process of setting of performance standards *must* consider the intended use of the standards. CLA standards established using the procedures outlined in this report are not designed to be used for selection purposes or as cut points for high-stakes assessment. They are designed to supplement the CLA value-added information to schools and provide feedback on performance to students. They are intended for use as further interpretation of CLA scores only.

---

[13] Though the CLA was not designed as an individual-level assessment tool, it could be used for individual-level assessment if it is one of several assessments being used to evaluate the individual.

Sixth, this report focused only on setting standards for the CLA PTs, because student responses on the new CLA MAs and BAs were not yet available. However, if schools pursue setting standards for the CLA, PTs are only half of the picture. As discussed previously, the CLA uses a matrix sampling approach in which each student completes either a PT or an MA and BA. For this reason, an individual does not have scores for all three measures. Although student performance could be considered in a compensatory fashion for the MAs and BAs, we would suggest setting standards for each separately and examining whether students meet expectations on one relative to the other. In other words, the process described for PTs should be repeated separately for the MAs and separately for the BAs. We would then advise that schools consider each aspect of performance relative to the standards corresponding to the relevant task type. This would provide greater diagnostic information than if the tasks were treated as compensatory and compared to a single standard across all three CLA task types.

Although the standard-setting methodology described here could be similarly applied to the MA and BA tasks, it has not been tested on those task types. The only difference that we would anticipate for those task types is a slight reduction in the time required to review each response, because responses for the MAs and BAs take less time to score. Nevertheless, there could be unanticipated differences that would require slight adjustments to the methodology; therefore, we advise schools to conduct pilot tests of the method to identify any obstacles unique to the MA and BA task types.

In sum, this study demonstrated a technique that can be used to set standards for college student performance on the CLA. The criteria for evaluating standard-setting studies presented in Chapter 2, along with the documentation of our method, results, and conclusions, is intended to provide schools with a set of guidelines for designing their own standard-setting study for the CLA. We hope this technique for establishing standards, in combination with descriptions of the characteristics of the various score ranges, will prove useful in further clarifying the meaning of CLA scores and providing feedback to students and faculty.

A. SAMPLE PERFORMANCE TASK SCREEN SHOTS: CRIME

CRIME: INTRODUCTION

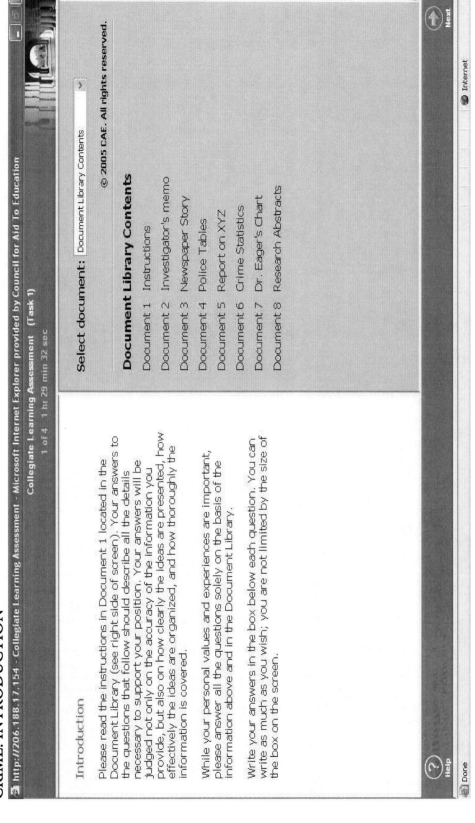

CRIME: QUESTION 1

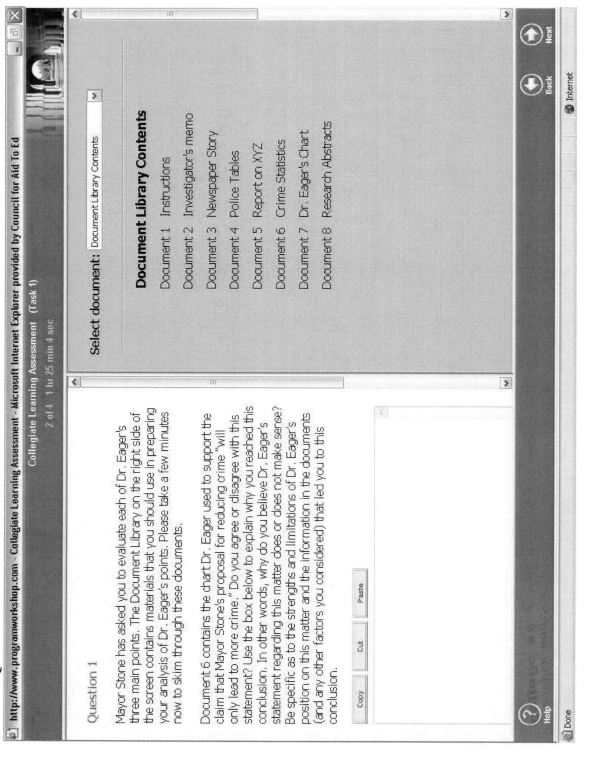

CRIME: QUESTION 2

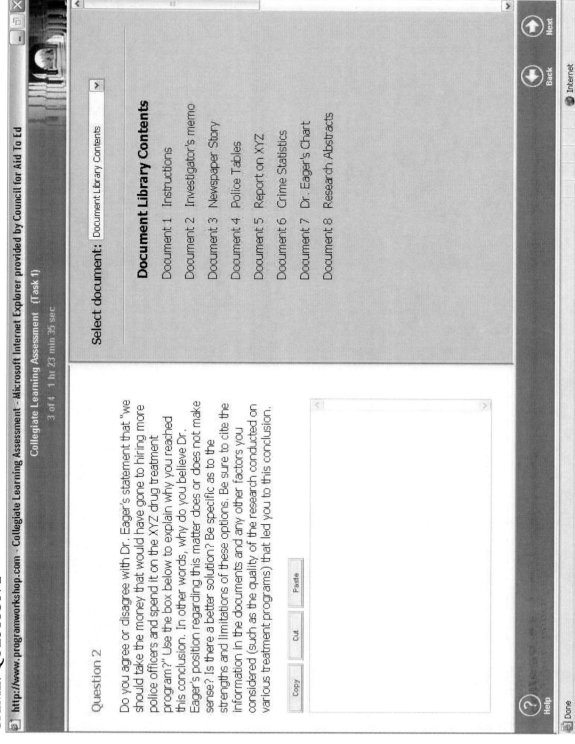

http://www.programworkshop.com - Collegiate Learning Assessment - Microsoft Internet Explorer provided by Council for Aid To Ed

Collegiate Learning Assessment   (Task 1)

3 of 4   1 hr 23 min 35 sec

Select document: Document Library Contents

Document Library Contents

Document 1   Instructions

Document 2   Investigator's memo

Document 3   Newspaper Story

Document 4   Police Tables

Document 5   Report on XYZ

Document 6   Crime Statistics

Document 7   Dr. Eager's Chart

Document 8   Research Abstracts

Question 2

Do you agree or disagree with Dr. Eager's statement that "we should take the money that would have gone to hiring more police officers and spend it on the XYZ drug treatment program?" Use the box below to explain why you reached this conclusion. In other words, why do you believe Dr. Eager's position regarding this matter does or does not make sense? Is there a better solution? Be specific as to the strengths and limitations of these options. Be sure to cite the information in the documents and any other factors you considered (such as the quality of the research conducted on various treatment programs) that led you to this conclusion.

Copy   Cut   Paste

Help   Back   Next

Done   Internet

CRIME: QUESTION 3

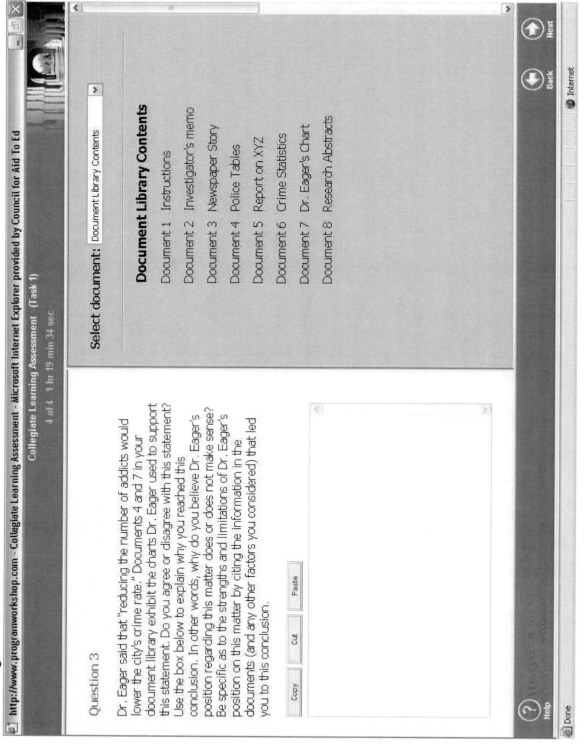

http://www.programworkshop.com - Collegiate Learning Assessment - Microsoft Internet Explorer provided by Council for Aid To Ed

Collegiate Learning Assessment   (Task 1)

4 of 4   1 hr 19 min 34 sec

Question 3

Dr. Eager said that "reducing the number of addicts would lower the city's crime rate." Documents 4 and 7 in your document library exhibit the charts Dr. Eager used to support this statement. Do you agree or disagree with this statement? Use the box below to explain why you reached this conclusion. In other words, why do you believe Dr. Eager's position regarding this matter does or does not make sense? Be specific as to the strengths and limitations of Dr. Eager's position on this matter by citing the information in the documents (and any other factors you considered) that led you to this conclusion.

Copy   Cut   Paste

Select document: Document Library Contents

Document Library Contents

Document 1   Instructions

Document 2   Investigator's memo

Document 3   Newspaper Story

Document 4   Police Tables

Document 5   Report on XYZ

Document 6   Crime Statistics

Document 7   Dr. Eager's Chart

Document 8   Research Abstracts

Help   Back   Next

Done   Internet

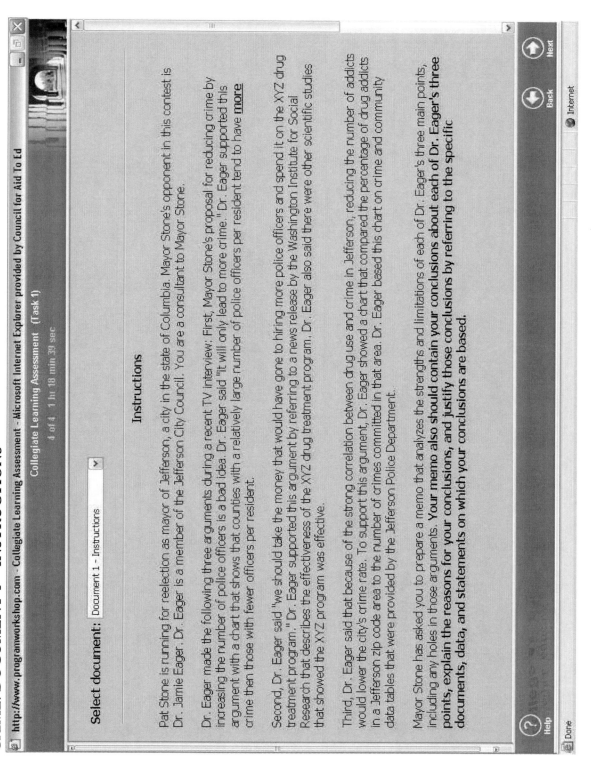

http://www.programworkshop.com - Collegiate Learning Assessment - Microsoft Internet Explorer provided by Council for Aid To Ed

Collegiate Learning Assessment (Task 1)

4 of 4   1 hr 18 min 39 sec

Select document: Document 1 – Instructions

Instructions

Pat Stone is running for reelection as mayor of Jefferson, a city in the state of Columbia. Mayor Stone's opponent in this contest is Dr. Jamie Eager. Dr. Eager is a member of the Jefferson City Council. You are a consultant to Mayor Stone.

Dr. Eager made the following three arguments during a recent TV interview: First, Mayor Stone's proposal for reducing crime by increasing the number of police officers is a bad idea. Dr. Eager said "it will only lead to more crime." Dr. Eager supported this argument with a chart that shows that counties with a relatively large number of police officers per resident tend to have **more** crime then those with fewer officers per resident.

Second, Dr. Eager said "we should take the money that would have gone to hiring more police officers and spend it on the XYZ drug treatment program." Dr. Eager supported this argument by referring to a news release by the Washington Institute for Social Research that describes the effectiveness of the XYZ drug treatment program. Dr. Eager also said there were other scientific studies that showed the XYZ program was effective.

Third, Dr. Eager said that because of the strong correlation between drug use and crime in Jefferson, reducing the number of addicts would lower the city's crime rate. To support this argument, Dr. Eager showed a chart that compared the percentage of drug addicts in a Jefferson zip code area to the number of crimes committed in that area. Dr. Eager based this chart on crime and community data tables that were provided by the Jefferson Police Department.

Mayor Stone has asked you to prepare a memo that analyzes the strengths and limitations of each of Dr. Eager's three main points, including any holes in those arguments. **Your memo also should contain your conclusions about each of Dr. Eager's three points, explain the reasons for your conclusions, and justify those conclusions by referring to the specific documents, data, and statements on which your conclusions are based.**

Help   Back   Next

Done   Internet

CRIME: DOCUMENT 2 – INVESTIGATOR'S MEMO

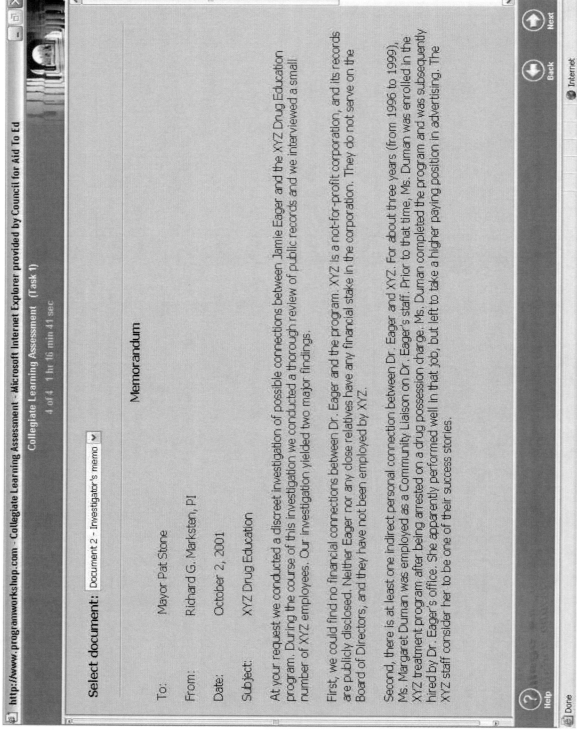

Select document: Document 2 - Investigator's memo

Memorandum

To: Mayor Pat Stone

From: Richard G. Marksten, PI

Date: October 2, 2001

Subject: XYZ Drug Education

At your request we conducted a discreet investigation of possible connections between Jamie Eager and the XYZ Drug Education program. During the course of this investigation we conducted a thorough review of public records and we interviewed a small number of XYZ employees. Our investigation yielded two major findings.

First, we could find no financial connections between Dr. Eager and the program. XYZ is a not-for-profit corporation, and its records are publicly disclosed. Neither Eager nor any close relatives have any financial stake in the corporation. They do not serve on the Board of Directors, and they have not been employed by XYZ.

Second, there is at least one indirect personal connection between Dr. Eager and XYZ. For about three years (from 1996 to 1999), Ms. Margaret Duman was employed as a Community Liaison on Dr. Eager's staff. Prior to that time, Ms. Duman was enrolled in the XYZ treatment program after being arrested on a drug possession charge. Ms. Duman completed the program and was subsequently hired by Dr. Eager's office. She apparently performed well in that job, but left to take a higher paying position in advertising. The XYZ staff consider her to be one of their success stories.

Help   Back   Next

Done   Internet

Select document: [Document 3 - Newspaper Story]

September 21, 2001

Jefferson Daily Press

Smart-Shop Robbery Suspect Caught

Drug-Related Crime on the Rise in Jefferson

Ann McNichols, Jefferson Township

On Monday police arrested a man suspected of robbing the Smart-Shop grocery store of $125. The arrest came less than six hours after J. Kim, the owner of the Smart-Shop store, reported the robbery. The suspect, David Kelso, was found just a few blocks from the store and he put up no resistance when police arrested him. He was apparently high on drugs he had purchased with some of the money taken from the store. Mr. Kim told reporters that Kelso came into the store just after it opened and demanded all the money from the cash register. He threatened the owner with a knife, and Mr. Kim gave him all the cash he had. The suspect fled, and Mr. Kim called the police.

A few hours later police responded to a telephone complaint and found David Kelso in an alley a few blocks from the store. The arresting officer said he appeared to be stoned and did not attempt to evade arrest. The officers found a syringe and other drug paraphernalia in Kelso's pocket. He was charged with armed robbery and possession of drugs.

This is the fifteenth drug-related arrest in Jefferson this month, and the police are calling it an epidemic. Sergeant Hugh Morris said "Drugs are now the number one law enforcement problem in Jefferson. Half of our arrests involve drugs." Mayor Stone has called for more money to hire more police officers to reduce the growing crime rate in Jefferson. But the Council is divided on what to do. City Councilmen Slater and Cohn called a press conference to demand that the rest of the council support an increase in the police budget. "If we put more cops on the street," they said, "we will show that criminals are not welcome in Jefferson." Mayoral candidate Dr. Jamie Eager called for a different approach. "More police won't make a difference, we need more drug treatment programs," Eager said. "The problem is not crime, per se, but crimes committed by drug users to feed their habits. Treat the drug use, and the crime will go away." The Council is slated to debate the proposed budget increase for police at its next meeting.

Next   Back

Help

Done   Internet

- 64 -

CRIME: DOCUMENT 4 – POLICE TABLES

CRIME AND DRUG USE IN JEFFERSON

The Jefferson Police Department prepared the two tables below for the city's five zip code areas. The percentage of drug users in the population was obtained from a survey. The middle column of Table 1 shows the number of robberies and burglaries that were reported to the Jefferson Police Department in 2000. The number of residents (i.e., homeowners and renters) and the percentage who are college graduates is based on 2000 US Census Bureau counts. The percentage of offenders living in a Jefferson zip code area who are drug users was based on drug tests of those arrested in 2000.

Table 1: Crime Statistics

Zip Code	Percentage of adults who are drug users	Number of robberies and burglaries	Number of residents	Number of robberies and burglaries per 1,000 residents
11510	1	172	20,018	8.59
11511	3	210	25,043	8.39
11512	5	271	29,978	9.04
11520	8	304	35,811	8.49
11522	10	322	37,501	8.59

Table 2: Demographic Characteristics

Zip Code	Percentage of offenders living in Jefferson who are drug users	Percentage of residents who are college graduates
11510	60	22
11511	50	16
11512	40	11
11520	35	9
11522	45	3

CRIME: DOCUMENT 5 – REPORT ON XYZ

Research Brief

Washington Institute for Social Research

XYZ drug treatment works in Clarendon

Clarendon is a typical small city in which a very un-typical event has occurred. An aggressive drug treatment effort is working to reduce the incidence of drug use.

Three years ago the city expanded its drug treatment program, nearly tripling the number of spaces available for drug users. Rather than continuing with the home-grown program operated by the health department, they contracted with XYZ Drug Treatment to launch a new effort. A recent survey has indicated that most everyone in Clarendon is happy with the new program.

Reported Incidence of drug use has dropped by 34% since the program began. The program has had its greatest impact on the use of crack cocaine, which surveys show has dropped 41% in three years. Furthermore, the crime rate has come down. During the past three years there have been fewer robberies, burglaries and assaults. These are crimes that are often associated with drug use. The drop in the rates for these crimes is a great as 25%.

XYZ Drug Treatment was founded by researchers from the University of Plymouth and Northside University. It began operations in Plymouth in 1990 focusing on a single neighborhood near one of the university campuses. The program was so successful in this neighborhood that it was expanded to cover the whole city.

The program uses a combination of approaches but focuses on social networks and their influence on drug use. Participants engage in group therapy, individual consultation, and outreach to their own peer group. Gent Dilfor, the founder of the program, says that research demonstrates that a high proportion of drug use is a social phenomenon, growing out of peer pressure and negative group norms. By attacking those features directly, XYZ helps the drug user address the factors that are likely to lead back into drug use.

The results in Clarendon confirm the wisdom of this approach. Not only is overall drug use down in the city, but repeat use is down even further. Those who complete the treatment stay off drugs longer than the national average, and many of the original participants appear to be drug-free two years later.

Help   Back   Next

Done   Internet

CRIME: DOCUMENT 6 – CRIME STATISTICS

http://www.programworkshop.com - Collegiate Learning Assessment - Microsoft Internet Explorer provided by Council for Aid To Ed

Collegiate Learning Assessment (Task 1)

2 of 4   1 hr 16 min 37 sec

Select document: Document 6 - Crime Statistics

State of Columbia
Department of Public Safety

Crime Statistics by County: 2000

The figure below shows the relationship between the number of police officers per 1,000 residents in a county and the incidence of robberies and burglaries in that county.

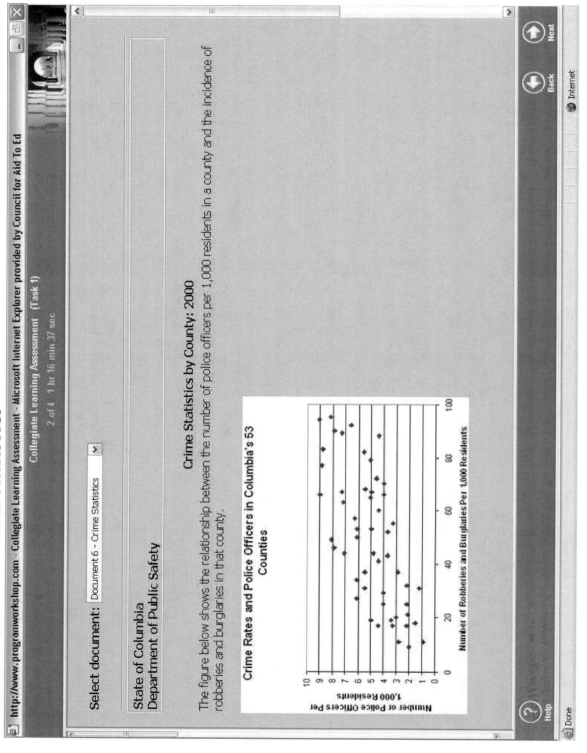

Crime Rates and Police Officers in Columbia's 53 Counties

Help   Back   Next

Done   Internet

CRIME: DOCUMENT 7 – DR. EAGER'S CHART

http://www.programworkshop.com - Collegiate Learning Assessment - Microsoft Internet Explorer provided by Council for Aid To Ed

Collegiate Learning Assessment   (Task 1)

2 of 4   1 hr 15 min 38 sec

Select document: Document 7 – Dr. Eager's Chart

DR. EAGER'S CHART

Dr. Eager used the chart below during the TV interview to show the relationship between the number of crimes committed and drug use in Jefferson.   This chart is based on data that were provided to Dr. Eager by the Jefferson City Police Department.

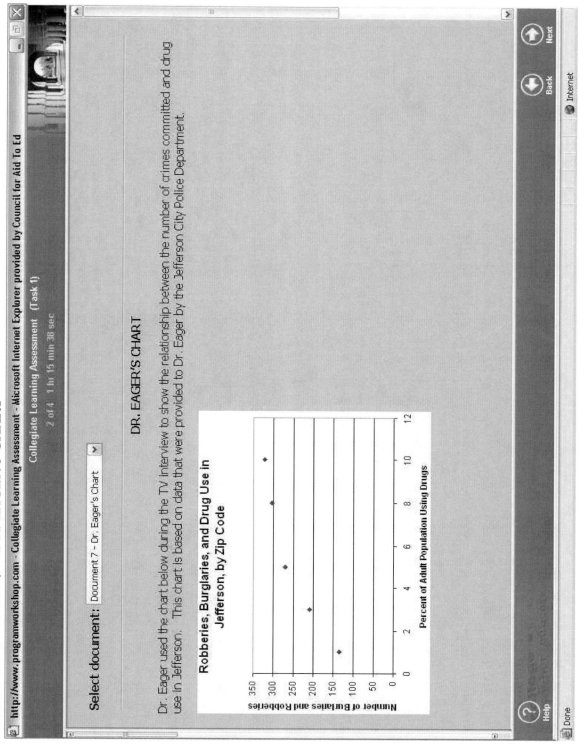

Robberies, Burglaries, and Drug Use in Jefferson, by Zip Code

Help   Back   Next

Done   Internet

CRIME: DOCUMENT 8 – RESEARCH ABSTRACTS

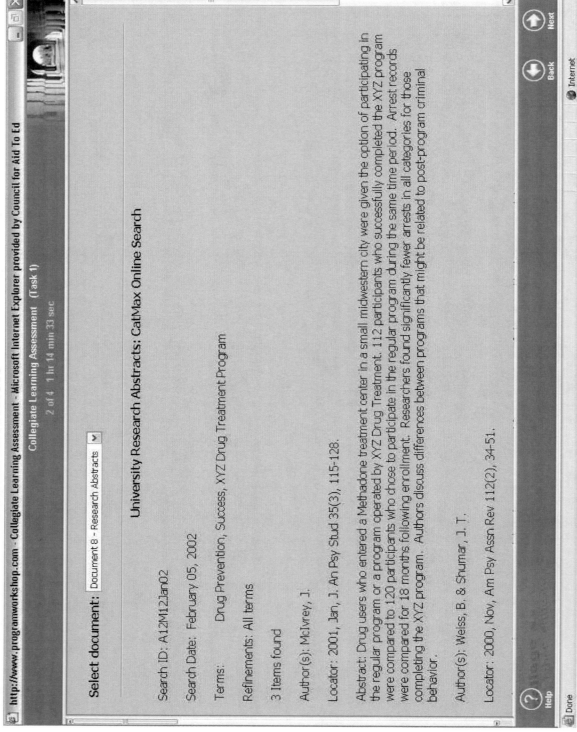

http://www.programworkshop.com - Collegiate Learning Assessment - Microsoft Internet Explorer provided by Council for Aid To Ed

Collegiate Learning Assessment   (Task 1)
2 of 4   1 hr 14 min 33 sec

Select document: Document 8 – Research Abstracts

University Research Abstracts: CatMax Online Search

Search ID: A12M12Jan02

Search Date: February 05, 2002

Terms: Drug Prevention, Success, XYZ Drug Treatment Program

Refinements: All terms

3 Items found

Author(s): McIvrey, J.

Locator: 2001, Jan, J. An Psy Stud 35(3), 115-128.

Abstract: Drug users who entered a Methadone treatment center in a small midwestern city were given the option of participating in the regular program or a program operated by XYZ Drug Treatment. 112 participants who successfully completed the XYZ program were compared to 120 participants who chose to participate in the regular program during the same time period. Arrest records were compared for 18 months following enrollment. Researchers found significantly fewer arrests in all categories for those completing the XYZ program. Authors discuss differences between programs that might be related to post-program criminal behavior.

Author(s): Weiss, B. & Shumar, J. T.

Locator: 2000, Nov, Am Psy Assn Rev 112(2), 34-51.

Help   Back   Next

Done   Internet

CRIME: DOCUMENT 8 – RESEARCH ABSTRACTS (CONT.)

Abstract: Drug users who entered a Methadone treatment center in a small midwestern city were given the option of participating in the regular program or a program operated by XYZ Drug Treatment. 112 participants who successfully completed the XYZ program were compared to 120 participants who chose to participate in the regular program during the same time period. Arrest records were compared for 18 months following enrollment. Researchers found significantly fewer arrests in all categories for those completing the XYZ program. Authors discuss differences between programs that might be related to post-program criminal behavior.

Author(s): Weiss, B. & Shumar, J. T.

Locator: 2000, Nov, Am Psy Assn Rev 112(2), 34-51.

Abstract: Subjects were 150 adults who were arrested for possession of drugs and had no prior adult arrests or convictions. Subjects who agreed to participate in the study were randomly assigned to one of two drug treatment programs or to no treatment. Clean House used group and family counseling. XYZ Drug Treatment used a social influence model. Subjects reported to researchers every three months for one year, and their arrest and hospitalization records were obtained. Offenders who completed their assigned treatment program had fewer arrests per person than the no treatment group. There were no significant differences between the Clean House and XYZ Drug Treatment participants on any of the post-treatment measures. Total costs for the two treatment programs were almost equal, but more offenders completed the Clean House program than completed the XYZ program.

Author(s): Penderton, M, Penderton, J. & Civic, T

Locator: 1999, May, J Psy Meth 12(1), 15-18.

Abstract: Research was conducted in the student health center of a large community college. Students with drug problems were randomly assigned to XYZ Drug Treatment or to the I Can treatment program. Subjects were followed for six months after referral and data were obtained about drug use, college grades, and arrests. Over a three-year period, 74 students were referred to XYZ and 78 to I Can. Approximately 20% of the students assigned to either program never reported for a single session. Of those who did report, over a quarter dropped out before completing the program. The dropout percentages were 27% for XYZ and 30% for I Can. After six months there were no differences between the two programs on any of the outcome measures studied.

End of search

Help   Back   Next

Done   Internet

B. LOW-, MID-, AND HIGH-LEVEL CRIME RESPONSES

LOW-LEVEL RESPONSES

CRIME QUESTION 1

I believe that what Dr. Eager is trying to say is that he want to improve the situation by going to the main source which is the drugs. To him he wants to help the drug users by submitting them to a rehibition program, and he feels that hiring more police officers will cost more, people will be getting taxed more, and jails will be filled more.

CRIME QUESTION 2

In my opinion I will agree Dr. Eager point I think we should use the money to spend it on the program and see what the outcome of the situation will like. If more drug users are serious about them getting help then the more the program will be more effient, but if the results are the opposite then the should be more officers in the city.

CRIME QUESTION 3

I agree with statement because to me the less users the less robberies.

CRIME QUESTION 1

Dr. Eager's proposal will lead to decrease in crime because criminals will be afraid of being caught as more police officers will be available. More available police officers can do their job better than less police officers. Each officer can concentrate on their specific area.

CRIME QUESTION 2

Police officers are required to hire in order to find people who are drug addicts. We cannot stop hiring police officers, but can reduce the number of hiring position so that more money can go into treatment of XYZ drug program. As document 5 says that drug addict people lead to increase in crime rate is very true. Treatment of drug addicts is very important to reduce the crime and hiring new police officers is also important at same level. Money for drug treatment can be taken out from any other area rather than from that spend in hiring police officers.

CRIME QUESTION 3

I think that the most crimes are done by drug addicts. When they require to take drug, most of the time they don't have money, so they rob or kill people for that. That is why it is very important to reduce drug addicts in order to reduce crimes.

CRIME QUESTION 1

Dr. eager has a good point for his first point to reduce the crime rate by hiring more police officers because more area can be covered and the police can go under cover and bust more people although there are some bad police officers. The second point is also good because if there are less addicts on the street there is less money to be made by dealers and less robberies and burgleries committed by addicts.

CRIME QUESTION 2

I think that money should go toward both causes because i believe both ideas will work.

CRIME QUESTION 3

I believe Dr. Eager is right about the crime rate compared to the number of addicts because according to the chart the crime rate goes up with the number of addicts.

CRIME QUESTION 1

I agree with the statement because you have to have statistics before you have have facts. By reading the statistics, you'll have a better understanding of your facts.

CRIME QUESTION 2

I disagree because later on down the line, yo might need some extra help and need to do some rehiring. A better solution would be to not spend so much money on the drug treatment, and make sure you have enough faculty to get the job done. If you get over staffed, then you can take some of the money from the hiring program and give it to the drug treatment program.

CRIME QUESTION 3

I disagree. A lot of people in the world that commit crime has a variety of reasons. For example, if someone wants to rob a store, that doesn't mean they are an addict, then just might need some quick cash and fell on hard times. If some commits a murder, that doesn't mean they are a addict, they just could be going through some psycholgical issues.

CRIME QUESTION 1

My feedback on Dr. Eager's three main points on crime control in Jefferson, Columbia:

I don't agree that hiring more law enforcement personnel would only lead to more crime. I think when properly implemented it is a positive step toward crime control. I think addressing drug trafficing over the borders is an important strategy and should be high in priority to stopping crime.

I do agree that more drug rehab programs should be in place and that targeting drug trafficing and addiction is key to reducing crime, but I also believe that attacking the cause is more effective than attacking just the symptom which is chronic substance abuse and addiction.

CRIME QUESTION 2

No. According to investigation performed by Richard G. Marksten, PI, that neither Dr. Eager nor any of his family are financially involved in the support of this non-profit program. So, I am not convinced by his lack of personal support of the program that the monies would be implimented as he proposes. I don't feel that taking money away from hiring more police officers is a good solution.

CRIME QUESTION 3

According to the statistics in Doc 4, I find it alarming that only a very miniscule percentage of adults are actual drug users. This would cause me to question how many crimes are committed by juveniles. It would seem to me that the percentage could very well be higher! Also, what percentage of drug users are college graduates?

According to Doc 5, it is clearly evident that wisely implemented drug rehab programs are effective in lowering drug use and reducing the numbers of drug-related crimes, particularly near college campuses and demographics of younger generations that are more likely to be attracted to drug use.

CRIME QUESTION 1

Well according to Document 5 - Report on XYZ, the crime rate went down with the treatment of XYZ. With the treatment of the people using drugs, the article says that the crime rate has gone down. "During the past three years there have been fewer robberies, burglaries and assaults. These are crimes that are often associated with drug use. The drop in the rates for these crimes is as great as 25%." This tells me that the program works. So I agree that there will be less crime if the program, XYZ, is implemented. I don't agree, or rather, don't understand the comment, "reducing crime will only lead to more crime." That doesn't make sense to me. A reduction in crime will be a reduction in crime...not an increase. Does this mean that by reducing crime that people will want to do more crimes? That just doesn't make sense. Dr. Eager makes a good point about the drug rehabilitation making a difference in crime rates. It makes sense that you would take away the crime and that will lead to a decrease in the crime...but to take away the crime and there be MORE crime, doesn't make sense.

CRIME QUESTION 2

I think the money should be split in half. I think the drug program should be given a chance. It isn't a bad idea. "The program uses a combination of approaches but focuses on social networks and their influence on drug use. Participants engage in group therapy, individual consultation, and outreach to their own peer group...research demonstrates that a high proportion of drug use is a social phenomenon, growing out of peer pressure and negative group norms. By attacking those features directly, XYZ helps the drug user address the factors that are likely to lead back into drug use." This kind of program should be given a chance.

CRIME QUESTION 3

Well if the crimes are being commited by the drug addicts, reducing the number of addicts would, in theory, lower the crime rate. The newspaper story says it all. The crime was commited by someone that was doped up on drugs. If that person was commited to the XYZ program, this crime probably wouldn't have happened. Now that the crime has been commited, the robber can now be admitted to the program and start on rehab. "This is the fifteenth drug-related arrest in Jefferson this month." If the arrestees would be put into the program, the crime rate would go down.

CRIME QUESTION 1

I agree that reducing crime will only lead to more crime. Government officials are trying so hard to eliminate crime that they are forgetting many criminals like the chase. A lot of criminal actions are done because they give the criminal a "high," trying to restrict crime will only make it harder to commit the crime but in turn cause a bigger high for the criminal once the crime had been committed.

There are two reasons why I believe that Dr. Eager's statement of more restrictions equals more crime makes sense. The first is the pure fact that it is near impossible to restrict crime. Crime will happen no matter how hard you try to stop it. Crimes happen in the littlest of places. For example, in the newspaper article. The man who stole the money from the shop had a syringe and other drug paraphernalia in his pocket, had he not been so doped up when he was caught he could have easily gotten away with the burglary and the even smaller crime, which was the drugs in his pocket. The other reason is again, the fact that the harder it is to commit a crime the more a criminal wants to do it.

I believe Dr. Eager is right to question the Mayor, because in all actuality we live in a world of crime. No matter how hard one tries, one person is not going to end the crimes.

CRIME QUESTION 2

I do agree with Dr. Eager's idea that we should use the money for an XYZ drug treatment center instead of hiring more police officers. Many crimes committed are committed because the person was either high or committing the crime to get money so they could in turn get high.

Even if the mayor was to add one hundred more police officers, so many crimes go unnoticed that it would not help anyways. At least a drug rehabilitation center would come in handy, because many of the unnoticed crimes are drug related. For example, methamphetamine labs and marijuana crops. Hiring more police officers than needed would just be a waste of money, which is most likely tax payer's money.

The report on XYZ stated that the use of drugs had dropped by 34%. Which in turn lowered the rate of crimes committed by 25%, because the report states that crimes such as, robberies, burglaries, and assaults are committed because of drug use. That statement proves that Dr. Eager's plan is a sure way to lower crime numbers.

Dr. Eager's statement makes sense because a lot of people are willing to stop their drug use. They are willing to stop because they realize it is hurting them and their families. Committing crimes while high, like a burglary, in their minds is not hurtful. So I think once they are off the drugs they will realize eveything they were doing, like burglarizing, was hurting them also.

CRIME QUESTION 3

I agree with this statement. It makes sense because in the Report on XYZ it stated that once the drug rate dropped so did the crime rate.

It is also proven in Document 7, the bigger the percentage of drug users the more robberies and burglaries were committed. The crime statistics in document 4 also prove this theory. The more drug users the more crimes.

The mayor should spend his time trying to figure out how to end drug problems, because that will begin to end the crime rate.

CRIME QUESTION 1

I agree with Mayor Stone becasue it is true. If you have more officers partolling Jefferson, burglers and other people who cause trouble will try to find new ways to get things done. They know that almost all of the cops are going to be looking at the places where they get more 'action' and where all the crime is happening. Anyways, even if you do hire more cops, drug addict are going to find new ways of getting money for their drugs, you cant get around that.

Money for a drug rehab will affect the community. Less people are going to buy drug and there got the convinient store robberies. The XYZ drug is doing wonders in a small city, the drug consumption has dropped 41% (Washington Institute for Social Research). This drug has had good effects on this small city and I think that it will also work in Jefferson.

CRIME QUESTION 2

I agree with Dr. Eager's statement, we should invest money on the XYZ Drug treatment program. It worked wonders in a small city and I believe that if this treatment is operated right it should work. We might not see a 41% increase becasue that was a small city and 41% would be a lot of people in a big city. We musnt get our hope down that Jefferson can be a place where drug is a minor issue. What I am trying to sya is that if we hiree more cops then we still havent solved the drug issue. We should solve the drug issue first and that is why I belive that we should spend more money on a drug rehab program than spending that money to hire new officers.

CRIME QUESTION 3

I believe that reducing the number of addicts would lower the crime rate becasue many people who are drug addicts will stop at nothing to get the money they need to get their stuff. Almost all of the iteams at the local pawn shop are stolen goods used to get quick and easy cash for drugs. Convinient stores and your house are one of the easiest wasys of getting quick cash. If you take all of the people caught becasue of stealing to get drug money and put them in a rehab center, I bet that most of them will not use drugs anymore. Yeah there might be a few that the program did not help but atleast there are less pepole in the street stealing for drugs. Cladendon didn't go and hire more officers, all they did was give to XZY drug program a chance and they dropped in crime rate and drug rates.

MID-LEVEL RESPONSES

CRIME QUESTION 1

I disagree with Dr. Eager's statement that more police officers will lead to more crime. At first glance, it would seem to a viewer in the general public that his claim is well-supported because of the data he provides. He states that more officers will only lead to more crime and then provides a graph which indeed shows that as the number of officers per resident increases, the number of crimes also seems to increase.

However, if one looks beyond the face value of this argument, the weaknesses become apparent. There are other things that need to be taken into consideration in order to use this data as support. The total population of each county, number of urban areas, and demographic information has a lot to do with the crime rate. A county that has few police officers may also have a smaller population, fewer cities, and more families or elderly residents; in such a case, the number of police officers does little to factor into the equation of total crime. On the same token, a county with a higher number of police officers per resident may also have more cities and a population that includes more people in low income brackets, unemployed residents, and a demographic group that is more likely to commit crimes. This deeper analysis of the data provided leads me to conclude that Dr. Eager's statement is not true.

CRIME QUESTION 2

Dr. Eager's position on this matter makes sense, but there could be a better solution besides using all the money for a drug treatment program or all of the money for more police officers. A compromise between the two approaches could be the best combination to combat both crime and drug use in Jefferson.

The reports on the XYZ Drug Treatment program do indicate that it is an effective program to treat drug users and consequently reduce crime rates and incidence of repeat use after completion of the program. The tables of crime and demographic statistics indicate a definite correlation between drug use and crime in Jefferson, but this does not mean that treating drug use would eliminate crime, nor does it mean that increasing the number of police officers would increase crime.

The research abstracts for studies comparing XYZ to other treatments programs indicate that in 2 of the 3 abstracts included here, other programs were just as effective as XYZ with no differences in percentage significant enough to judge which one was more effective. Hiring some police officers who have special training or expertise in the area of drug-related crimes could be a beneficial move that would address both sides of the issue at hand. Using some of the money to improve Jefferson's existing treatment options and using the rest of it to add members of the police force that specialize in drug-related problems would be a viable solution.

CRIME QUESTION 3

Dr. Eager's statement that reducing the number of addicts would lower the city's crime rate makes a lot of sense. The charts he uses to demonstrate this are effective in showing this relationship, but there are some flaws in the way that the data is used.

In Table 1 of Crime Statistics, the data shows that as the percentage of the population who are drug users increases, the number of robberies and burglaries also increases. However, the number of residents for each zip code also increases along with this data. As the population of an area increases, other crime-causing factors increase as well. Poverty and economic unrest could also lead to increased drug use and thus increased crime. Dr. Eager's examination of the causal relationship between drugs and crime must also be accompanied by an investigation of what causes drug use to be higher in some areas. His argument would be strengthened if he could dig deeper and find out why drug use is more prevalent in some areas and perhaps addressing those issues is the best method of solution.

CRIME QUESTION 1

Dr. Eager's statement regarding how the number of officers per 1,000 residents affects crime. This statment is based on a chart that seems to suggest, that the more officers you have in an area, the higher the rate of crime in that area. But the study does not take into consideration that certian areas tend to have a larger crime rates. So the areas that have a larger crime rate, would be the areas that you would assign more officers to. It doesn't make sense that to assign a large number of officers to an area with a low amount of crime. The statement by Dr. Eager while accurate according to the data provided is fundamentaly flaw dew to the fact that all areas are not the same. So therefore you would not get the same results in each area by increasing or decreasing the police presence.

CRIME QUESTION 2

The XYZ drug treatment program seems to be effective in reducing the dependancey of drug users. While effective it is no more effective then the Clean House Treatment(Weiss and Shumar). The effectiveness of this program is in whether or not the subjects complete the program. When a use completes a drug program the user typically has a higher rate of sucess then users who do not complete a program(Weiss and Shumar). The recommendation would be to implement a drug treatment program. It does not need to be the XYZ program, but putting a program in place will reduce the number of drug related crimes by reducing the number of drug offenders.

CRIME QUESTION 3

Reducing the number of addicts would not bring the crime rate down. According to table on the percentage of users had no direct coralation to the number of drug related crimes comitted per resident. While reducing the number of users would be nice it has no real effect.

CRIME QUESTION 1

I feel that the statement made by Dr. Eager is an unfair assessment of the ability of the police based solely on one document which does not contain enough information to be sound. Since there are no other factors regarding the neighborhoods, socioeconomic status, or education levels of those residing there being taken into consideration, I feel that it is very irresponsible to imply that police officers are not capable of performing their jobs based on one chart. If you want to use one demographic to make a generalization, look at the Police Table on Crime and Drug use in Jefferson. In every zip code, the percentage of drug-using offenders lowers as the number of college graduates lowers. So, using this demographic, one can say that there are more drug users who are college graduates than there are in those who have not graduated from college. Neither a fair nor true generalization, but one that can be made from using just the one chart.

CRIME QUESTION 2

While I agree with Dr. Eager that treatment programs can be very beneficial, I do not necessarily agree that huge amounts of money should be invested on the XYZ drug treatment program. First of all, those who benefit from such programs have to want help...not do it because it is a better alternative than jail. As we learned from the research by Penderton, entering the program isn't enough. Many people who sign up for these programs don't complete them, and several never showed up at all. Therefore, just having this program in place CANNOT ensure its success not that of lowering crime rates.

CRIME QUESTION 3

While reducing the number of addicts may lower the city's crime rate, the demographics provided do not prove that. As stated earlier, there is not enough information regarding other factors that have the potential to influence crime rates to use this as supporting data. Drug treatment programs are wonderful and can be successful for those who want to make a change and are willing to put forth all the effort that is required, but there is not enough proof to warrant putting an enormous amount of money into a program that may work or could end up failing miserably.

CRIME QUESTION 1

I believe Dr.Eager's claim that Mayor Stones efforts to reduce crime by increasing the number of police officers will only serve to increase it to be inaccurate. For one thing, Ther is no possible way that obtaining more police officers can be linked to an acctual increase in the crime rate. Though the chart used by Dr. Eager to support his opinion does seem to indicate a conection between the number of officers and the rate of crime, it does not provide substansial evidence to support his claim. The chart only shows a link between the current number of polie and the crime rate. The counties that have both many police and high crime rates could possibly have hired extra police to cut down on the number of crimes that were already being committed. In order for this chart to be of an actual value, it would have to show the info for several years.

However, I think perhaps Dr. Eager might be onto something in his opinion about putting more money into drug treatment programs It is something we should comsider. There are tables that have been prepared by the Jefferson County Police Department which show that the percent of drug users is almost always linked to the crime rate. More drug use, more crime.

As far as it the xyz Drug program is concerned, I have come to the conclusion that while drug tretment programs may be a good thing to invest in, there is nothing to indicate that "xyz" would be better than any other one.

CRIME QUESTION 2

Taking all the money that was intentended to be spent on officers and instead using it to fund the xyz drug would not be the best option. Through much reseach, I have come to the conclusion that the best option would be to combine the efforts of the police with some type of drug program. Although police are a very vital part of our war against crime and drug use, incresing their numbers will not serve to eliminate the drug problem. In fact, a chart prepared by the State of Columbia Department of Public Safety shows that increasing the number of officers ussuually does not affect the crime rate at all, but can sometimes acctually have an inverse affect. In addition, studies that have been done show that individuals who complete a drug program seem to have a lower arrest rate than those who do not.

However, the xyz program does not appear to provide any particular advantage over the other drug programs availible

CRIME QUESTION 3

While the police tables that Dr. Eager used did show a higher number of crimes in areas that had a higher number of drug users, he failed to look at the acctual percentage. Those areas with a greater number of crimes commmitted also had a larger population; therefor the acttual proportion of crimes to drug users is not directly related. In fact, some areas acctually had less drug users and more crime. Thereby, the conclusion can be reached that while reducing the number of drug users would help our crime rate, it would not serve as a "end-all" solution. Other measures will still need to be taken.

HIGH-LEVEL RESPONSES

CRIME QUESTION 1

Dr. Eager's argument sounds appealing, but its gaping holes in logic and lack of proper consideration of all factors undermine its potency. Dr. Eager contends that increasing the number of police on the street "will only lead to more crime". The chart he uses to support this claim (Chart 6) does seem to support this theory if only quickly reviewed. However, if one actually takes the time to more deeply analyze the chart, it is apparent that this particular argument makes vast generalizations.

Consider first the region of the chart in which 20 robberies and burglaries are committed per 1,000 residents. There are at least 8 counties at that level of crime, yet the number of police officers per 1,000 residents varies from about 1,000 to 5,000 officers. Now, if Dr. Eager's argument were to be completely true, what would explain this similarity in the number of crimes committed in two counties when both have very different levels of police present? The fact that this question can be validly posed at nearly every level of crime serves to undermine the validity of Dr. Eager's broad argument.

It can be noted that of the counties with a higher police presence, many have higher crime rates as compared to those regions with smaller police forces. Yet, this does not support Dr. Eager's argument. He is trying to prove a correlation between crime and police, suggesting that more police bring about more crime. It seems more plausible to assume, however, that the level of police is reactionary and dependant upon the preexisting level of crime. If a certain county has more crime, then the police force needed to keep that crime in check will have to be larger. Factors that would contribute to this could include, but are not limited to population, socio-economic factors, and possibly drug-use, but none of these are the exclusive catalysts of crime.

CRIME QUESTION 2

Dr. Eager makes an interesting argument when he asserts that more money should be spent on the XYZ treatment program instead of enlarging the police force. Certainly, the case of XYZ's relative success in Clarendon (as cited by the Washington Institute for Social Research) indeed supports Eager's claim. The fact that Clarendon viewed a decrease in the crime rate when the XYZ drug treatment program opened its doors implies a correlation between drug use and crime. However as Document 5 explicitly states, "these are crimes that are OFTEN associated with drug use." The most one can take from this research brief is that crime and drug use decreased over a period of time in which XYZ was up and running. This could be coincidental or it could actually be a causal relationship, but there is not conclusive evidence to confirm any of those two ideas.

Document 4's police tables also serve to greatly undermine Dr. Eager's claim that money spent on extra police officers is not helping the crime issue. In Jefferson's 5 zip codes, while the number of crimes has increased as population increases, the relative percentages of crimes in these zip codes is about the same. The crime rate is generally proportional to the population. One can also assume that the number of police is also proportional to the population. So, in areas where more people reside, more crime occurs, and more police officers are needed to patrol the streets. This is a logical relationship that links all 3 factors being considered in this study. Dr. Eager's assumptions, however, try to draw a line between crime and the number of police, ignoring almost obvious observations concerning the data.

Spending higher sums of money on the XYZ treatment program appears to be somewhat fruitless - the program is reactionary and involves those who feel that they need help and seek to rehabiliate themselves at the center. However, XYX would play a relatively minor role in deterring crime by first-time offenders. It may very well have great success in helping out individuals who enter its doors, but how many criminals actually end up at the center before they commit their wrongdoings?

And if drug use plays such a huge role in determining the level of crime, then why is it that as the percentages of adults who are drugs users increases, the percentage of offenders living in Jefferson who are drug users decreases (Document 4). This does not necessarily imply that more drug users means less offenses on the their part, but it does at least show that one cannot make the assumption that more drug usage equals more crime on their part.

Programs that may have a more meaningful effect could possibly include stronger education programs for the city's youth and economic subsidies and tax incentives that help local business grow and compete. Education programs would help deter crime and drug use by providing children with a means for improving their lives without partaking in criminal behavior. If they believe that they can use their knowledge and intelligence to go out into the world and compete equally for jobs and opportunies, they will tend less toward crime then otherwise. As the local market becomes more successful, the relative wealth of Jefferson and its 5 zip codes will increase. If people think they have more of an opportunity to ascend the social ladder through legitimate means, they may be less inclined to commit crime.

The quality of the research in some of these sources is debatable considering the fact that many of those who joined the XYZ program joined by choice (as in McIvrey's and Weiss' book / Document 8). This could mean different levels in their enthusiasm to become rehabiliated. It could also have other ramifications that cannot directly be identified, but that cannot be ignored. When studies like this are carried out, it is important that the sample group share similar qualities to the general population beinge examined. If those studied chose XYZ or agreed to participate in the program after being explained its benefits, they are quite different from a sample group that was randomly chosen and observed with or without consent.

For these reasons, I find that Dr. Eager's argument for more money to be spent on the XYZ program is flawed.

CRIME QUESTION 3

Document 7, which exhibits Dr. Eager's own chart, correlates crime to the percent of the adult population using drugs. While it may seem to show a direct relationship between the two, it does not necessarily imply that one causes the other since it ignores important factors like population.

Document 4 strikes down Eager's argument in a heartbeat. He believes that "reducing the number of addicts would lower the city's crime rate". However, the crime rate is relatively stable among all 5 zip codes regardless of population. Moreover, when the percentage of adults who are drugs users increases from 1% in 11510 to 10% in 11522, the number of robberies and burglaries per 1,000 residents goes from 8.59% to 8.59%, exhibiting no change.

It is quite obvious to see that increasing drug usage does not mean more crime. Other factors possibly contribute even more heavily to the crime rate. These factors as mentioned before include the economic situation of the times, the level of education being provided to the people, the population of a certain region, and the ethnic/social make-up that could or could not lead to more intense race relations.

CRIME QUESTION 1

Dr. Eager's statement that increasing the Jefferson police department's budget "will only lead to more crime" is fallacious. At first glance, Document 6, a graph of the number of police officers per thousand residents against the number of robberies and burglaries per thousand residents, appears to lend credibility to this assertion, since the graph does show a small upward trend in robberies and burglaries as the number of police officers increases. However, the argument is largely unsubstantiated for a number of reasons.

First, Dr. Eager interprets the data as demonstrating a conclusive upward trend in crime as the number of police officers increases, whereas in fact the data are widely scattered. While there is a general upward trend in the number of robberies and burglaries as the number of police officers per thousand residents increases, the data are far from conclusive; in many cases, a county with more police officers than another has fewer crimes than that other county.

Second, Dr. Eager commits the fallacy of confusing correlation with causation. Document 6 does demonstrate a correlation between the number of police officers and the number of robberies and burglaries; however, this does not necessarily mean that the increase in police officers caused the increase in crime. In reality, it is more likely that the higher crime levels predated the increase in the size of the police force. Mayor Stone's proposal to add more officers is hardly new; it would be reasonable to assume that other government officials in other Columbia counties enacted similar proposals in the face of high crime rates.

Finally, the chart in Document 6 only gives data regarding the number of robberies and burglaries - a specific type of crime. It is entirely possible that, even if having more police officers in a city is statistically linked to higher robbery and burglary levels, a bigger police force is also linked to lower levels of rape, arson, and murder - clearly an equally important correlation. Thus, Dr. Eagle is incorrect to isolate the trend in burglaries and robberies and use it as a generalization for the trend in all crime as the police force varies in size.

CRIME QUESTION 2

Dr. Eager's statement that "we should take the money that would have gone to hiring more police officers and spend it on the XYZ drug treatment program" relies on two assumptions: first, that the proposed allocation for hiring more police officers would be wasted; and second, that the XYZ drug program is an effective solution to crime.

The first assumption, as addressed in Question 1, is flawed: the crime statistics show no definite causal relationship between increasing the number of police officers and increasing levels of crime, and it would be a mistake to abandon the option of enlarging the police force without a more detailed analysis of the likely impacts of doing so.

The second assumption, that the XYZ program is effective, is more defensible but nonetheless specious. Dr. Eager cites two references to back up her claim that the XYZ program works: first, a report by the Washington Institute for Social Research reproduced in Document 5; and second, "other scientific studies." The first is a press release specifically dealing with the effectiveness of the XYZ program in Clarendon, a small town. The second is an exaggeration: of the three studies summarized in Document 8, only one gives any ground to the claim that the XYZ program is more effective. (Indeed, another of the studies in Document 8 suggests that the XYZ program had a higher dropout rate than the Clean House program, to which XYZ was compared in the study.)

Taken together, these pieces of evidence are promising but not conclusive. The Washington Institute report constitutes only one case of a small town in which XYZ was successful; any number of differences between Jefferson and Clarendon might mean that the XYZ program would be much less effective in Jefferson. The 2001 McIvrey study in Document 8 is even more problematic. While it does conclude that the XYZ program seemed to have a greater deterrent effect on future arrests by program participants, the wording of the abstract suggests that the comparison may not be fair: "112 participants who successfully completed the XYZ program were compared to 120 participants who chose to participate in the regular program." While the wording is unclear, the abstract leaves open the possibility that successful graduates of the XYZ course were compared to participants who had dropped out of the regular drug treatment program - clearly an unfair comparison. Thus, even taken together, the study and the press release constitute insufficient evidence to justify a decision by the city of Jefferson to jettison proposals for increased police funds altogether and dedicate its money to the unproven XYZ program.

A better solution would ideally be based on further policy research. Many cities respond to drug-related crime epidemics by increasing the size of their police forces; any rational approach to public policy would benefit tremendously from examining the results of those decisions, particularly in cities demographically similar to Jefferreson. While the XYZ program still appears to be a viable option, none of the evidence presented here serves as a firm proof of its effectiveness; the city should allocate money to XYZ on a trial basis and increase funding if the program proves effective at addressing the specific needs of Jefferson. The complex nature of drug abuse as a social problem and a security challenge suggests that a multifacteted approach might be most effective; splitting resources between prevention and enforcement might be a better solution than either candidate's proposals.

CRIME QUESTION 3

While Dr. Eager may well be correct that reducing the number of addicts would lower the crime rate in Jefferson, the evidence she presents to support this claim does not confirm it. The primary evidence Dr. Eager uses is presented in Table 1 of Document 4, which shows the drug use rate, number of robberies and burglaries, and number of robberies and burglaries per thousand residents in various zip codes in Jefferson. Dr. Eager's graph in Document 7 shows a clear positive correlation between the percentage of adults who use drugs and the number of robberies and burglaries in a given zip code. However, the number of robberies and burglaries does not determine the crime rate, which is calculated as a ratio of crimes to residents. The table in Document 4 shows that the drug use rate does not necessarily correlate to the robbery and burglary rate; indeed, there appears to be no conclusive correlation, with the highest robbery and burglary rate corresponding to the median drug use rate. Additionally, the emphasis on robberies and burglaries alone fails to account for other crimes; Dr. Eager presents no evidence for the case that a lower drug use rate will decrease the rates of murder, rape, and other crimes.

CRIME QUESTION 1

Dr. Eager's claim that an increase in police officers "will only lead to more crime" is an absolutely outrageous statement, both in thought and given the actual statistics. Obviously, as long as the police officers do their job and so their job well, which we can only assume is true, an increase in police officers can only serve to better equip the community with resources necessary to fight and thereby reduce crime. Also, though the chart Dr. Eager uses to "prove" his point does show a positive correlation between the number of police officers per 1,000 and the number of robberies and burglaries per 1,000 residents, no conclusions can be deduced from it that would allow one to say that a rise in police officers causes a rise in robberies and burglaries. The correlation can be shown but the causation is nowhere to be found in what can be concluded out of this chart alone. A more likely conclusion to be made from the chart is that the more robberies and burglaries there are per capita, the more police officers that are necessary to maintain some sort of civilization in the district. As a result, Dr. Eager's position and statements are thoroughly false and make little intuitive sense.

CRIME QUESTION 2

At first glance, it looks as if this is a promising idea for many reasons. Dr. Eager has obviously done his research with the XYZ drug treatment program, given that it is one of his main platform points. He must be familiar with the Weiss, et al; Penderton, et al; and McIvrey studies on drug prevention success that all contain significant results that the XYZ program is at least as good, if not better in the case of the McIvrey study, than regular group and family counseling programs (Weiss, et al) or another program called I Can (Penderton, et al). Though the studies are for the most part fairly valid, the lack of random assignment may have been the reason for a higher success rate in the XYZ program of the McIvrey study. This does not diminish the fact, however, that the research brief of the Washington Institute for Social Reasearch shows at least a baseline efficacy, if not better, of the XYZ program. Furthermore, he has had first hand experience with a Ms. Margaret Duman who was considered to be a success story of the XYZ program and a competent employee of Dr. Eager's staff. All of this experience on the matter even led Dr. Eager to be so convinced that this was the right decision that he publicly announced the problem in the Jefferson Daily Press by saying, "more police won't make a difference, we need more drug treatment programs [...] The problem is not crime, per se, but crimes committed by drug users to feed their habits." Putting money into the XYZ program (allowing that Dr. Eager has no financial interest in the idea [Document 2]) seems like the best idea, but is it?

Ultimately, this may not be the most effective solution to the problem, again because Dr. Eager has ineffectively used the information at hand to attempt to prove his case that drug use causes increased robberies. By plotting the number of burglaries and robberies as a lump-value against the normalized percentage of the adult population using drugs, the graph only shows a positive correlation between the number of burglaries and robberies in their entirety and the percentage of the adult population using drugs. It would be invalid to point to causation from this chart as it does not say anything about the actual crime rate, only the instance of crime in its entirety, neglecting the difference in population size of each zip code area. A chart that more effectively shows what is actually going on would be one that plots the number of burglaries and robberies per 1,000 residents against the percent of the adult population using drugs. This chart would show that as the percent of the drug-using population increases, the number of burglaries and robberies per 1,000 residents actually stays relatively the same; the meaning that can be derived from such a chart would be that a higher proportion of the adult population using drugs actually does not lead to a higher crime rate.

Though the information only allows itself that the best option so far would probably be to increase the police task (even given Dr. Eager's objections), another possible solution would be to look into the college graduation rates of the areas. Overall percentages of college graduates have a negative correlation with the percentage of adults who are drug users. Also, the percentage of offenders who are drug users is relatively high in every zip code region. The root of the problem, therefore, may be that non-college graduates are more likely to develop drug habits, drug habits that may co-accompany, and on some level contribute to, the mindframe of an offender. The new money to enter the community might effectively reduce the crime rate if it was injected into programs designed to increase the college graduation rate of the community.

CRIME QUESTION 3

Dr. Eager's statement is two-sided and therefore hard to conclude which side is the most important to look at. First of all, the percentage of adult drug users seems not to affect the number of robberies and burglaries per 1,000 residents; this is something that does not come through in Dr. Eager's chart. By this token, reducing the number of addicts seems to not affect the crime rate much at all. On the other hand, offenders as compared to non-offenders have a disproportionately high rate of drug use, lending to the idea that there is a positive correlation between drug use and the propensity to become an offender. Ultimately, however, Dr. Eager's position is weak at best because his statistics cannot prove any correlation between drug use and the propensity to offend. The disproportionately high rate of drug use of offenders as compared to non-offenders could just point to the idea of co-morbidity, the same mind that has a high propensity to offend has a high propensity to become a drug user; in that respect, decreasing the amount of addicts may only have the result of decreasing the percentage of offenders who are drug users, not the number of robberies and burglaries per 1,000 residents or the crime rate itself. His argument would most likely make sense to the laymen, but anybody who could effectively read and make truly valid assumptions from the two documents that Dr. Eager presents can see that his statement has no logical ground on which to stand.

C. QUESTIONNAIRE ITEM AND SCALE MEANS AND STANDARD DEVIATIONS

Item Group	Cronbach's Alpha [a]	Mean Score	SD
Does the test measure an important educational construct?	.75 (.64)	4.49	.43
The type of performance measured by this test should be an important part of a student's course work.		4.40	.63
This performance task measures important skills college graduates should possess.		4.70	.53
Colleges should prepare students to do well on tasks like this.		4.40	.55
This test measures important skills all students should possess.		4.40	.55
College courses should NOT include tasks like this as homework or in-class exercises. (R)	Item dropped	1.70	1.03
Is this type of performance being measured or taught in college courses?	.67	2.78	.33
This task is similar to homework and exercises that students are given in college.		2.90	.93
College courses RARELY include tasks like this as homework or in class exercises. (R)		3.20	.87
Colleges do NOT work as hard as they should to improve performance on this type of task. (R)		3.80	.79
Does this measure what it is intended to measure (critical thinking skills, value-added, etc.)?	.55 (.48)	4.14	.46
Students do NOT need good writing skills to do well on this task. (R)		1.90	1.17
Students need good critical thinking skills to do well on this task.		4.60	.54
College seniors should perform better on this task than college freshmen.		4.70	.48
Most college seniors would perform well on this task.		3.10	.57
College courses prepare students to do well on this type of task.	Item dropped	3.00	.76
Does performance on the test predict important life outcomes?	.84	3.93	.62
Students who do poorly on this task would also perform poorly in a job requiring critical thinking.		4.10	.84

Students who do poorly on this task would also perform poorly in a job requiring good problem solving.		4.10	.81
This task is similar to situations students face in their day-to-day lives after college.		3.80	1.07
This task is NOT similar to situations students face in their careers after college. (R)		1.90	.91
Students who do well on this task would also perform well in a job requiring good written communication.		4.20	.83
Students who do well on this task would also perform well in a job requiring good decision-making.		4.10	.70
Students who do well on this task will also make sound decisions in their day-to-day lives.		3.20	.86
Would training people to do well on tasks like this help people get ahead in life?	.83	4.08	.66
Learning how to perform well on this type of task would help Americans compete in a global market.		4.20	.81
Learning how to perform well on this type of task would help a student get ahead in life.		4.00	.67
Learning how to perform well on this type of task would help U.S. college graduates make better political, economic, and social decisions for our country.		4.00	.80
How would known groups perform on this task?	.60 (.58)	3.76	.36
Most college professors would do well on this task.		3.90	.85
I would do well on this task.		4.30	.60
Most high school dropouts would do well on this task. (R)		1.80	.84
Most successful business executives would do well on this task.		3.70	.72
Most construction workers would do poorly on this task.		2.70	.83
Most freshmen college students would do well on this task. (R)		3.80	.61
Most plumbers would do poorly on this task.	Item dropped	2.40	.85

[a] Cronbach's alpha before the removal of the dropped items is presented in parentheses.

Note: all scale items are on a scale from 1 = strongly disagree to 5 = strongly agree. Items that are reverse-coded are noted by (R). Reverse-coded items show the original response mean before recoding for computing the total scale score means.

D. INDIVIDUAL AND GROUP STANDARD-SETTING RESULTS

Table D.1
Entering Freshman Cut Points for the Standards

	Adequate/Barely Acceptable Low Cutoff				Proficient/Clearly Acceptable Low Cutoff				Exemplary/Outstanding Low Cutoff			
	Range	Median	Mean	SD	Range	Median	Mean	SD	Range	Median	Mean	SD
Individual cut points												
Overall (*n*=41)	790 – 1150	880	**922**	95	970 – 1420	1150	**1130**	113	970 – 1600	1420	**1356**	131
by location:												
Santa Monica Panel (*n*=18)	790 – 1150	925	**940**	102	970 – 1330	1150	**1155**	103	970 – 1510	1420	**1375**	135
New York Panel (*n*=23)	790 – 1150	880	**907**	88	970 – 1420	1060	**1111**	118	1060 – 1600	1330	**1342**	128
by task:												
Brain Boost (*n*=9)	790 – 880	880	**850**	45	970 – 1240	1060	**1060**	96	970 – 1510	1330	**1300**	174
Crime (*n*=9)	970 – 1150	970	**1020**	79	1150 – 1330	1240	**1230**	84	1420 – 1510	1420	**1450**	45
Catfish (*n*=9)	880 – 1060	880	**910**	64	1060 – 1420	1150	**1150**	110	1240 – 1600	1330	**1360**	119
Lake to River (*n*=9)	790 – 1150	880	**920**	111	970 – 1330	1150	**1120**	101	1240 – 1510	1330	**1370**	79
Parks (NY only, *n*=5)	790 – 970	880	**898**	75	970 – 1150	1060	**1042**	75	1060 – 1420	1240	**1258**	161

Table D.1 cont.

Panel consensus cut points

	Range		Consensus	%	Range		Consensus	%	Range		Consensus	%
Overall (k=9)	880 - 1060	880	**939***	74	1060 - 1240	1150	**1139***	81	1240 - 1510	1420	**1389***	89
by location:												
Santa Monica Panel (k=4)	880 - 1060	925	**950**	79	1060 - 1240	1150	**1150**	69	1330 - 1510	1420	**1420**	69
New York Panel (k=5)	880 - 1060	880	**931**	71	1060 - 1240	1060	**1130**	90	1240 - 1510	1330	**1365**	97
by task:												
Brain Boost (k=2)	880	880	**880**	-	1060	1060	**1060**	-	1330	1330	**1330**	-
Crime (k=2)	1060	1060	**1060**	-	1240	1240	**1240**	-	1420 - 1510	1510	**1470**	47
Catfish (k=2)	880 - 970	970	**930**	47	1150 - 1240	1150	**1200**	47	1420 - 1510	1510	**1470**	47
Lake to River (k=2)	880 - 970	880	**920**	47	1060 - 1150	1150	**1100**	47	1330 - 1420	1330	**1370**	47
Parks (NY only, k=1)	880	880	**880**	-	1060	1060	**1060**	-	1240	1240	**1240**	-

*Suggested as final cut points for the standards.

Note: Number of panel members and number of groups are noted as n and k respectively.

- 99 -

Table D.2
Exiting Senior Cut Points for the Standards

Individual faculty cut points	Adequate/Barely Acceptable Low Cutoff				Proficient/Clearly Acceptable Low Cutoff				Exemplary/Outstanding Low Cutoff			
	Range	Median	Mean	SD	Range	Median	Mean	SD	Range	Median	Mean	SD
Overall (n=41)	880 - 1240	1060	1069	98	1060 - 1420	1330	1295	96	1330 - 1600	1510	1527	72
by location:												
Santa Monica Panel (n=18)	970 - 1240	1060	1075	89	1150 - 1420	1330	1305	74	1330 - 1600	1510	1536	69
New York Panel (n=23)	880 - 1240	1060	1064	107	1060 - 1420	1330	1287	111	1330 - 1600	1510	1519	75
by task:												
Brain Boost (n=9)	970 - 1150	1060	1030	64	1150 - 1330	1240	1260	75	1330 - 1600	1510	1521	89
Crime (n=9)	1060 - 1240	1150	1150	64	1330 - 1420	1420	1380	47	1510 - 1600	1600	1580	40
Catfish (n=9)	970 - 1240	1060	1060	110	1060 - 1420	1240	1270	119	1330 - 1600	1510	1490	75
Lake to River (n=9)	880 - 1240	970	1030	110	1150 - 1330	1240	1260	75	1420 - 1600	1510	1510	45
Parks (NY only, n=5)	970 - 1240	1060	1078	99	1150 - 1420	1330	1312	117	1420 - 1600	1600	1540	104

Table D.2 cont.

Panel consensus cut points

Overall (*k*=9)	970 - 1240	1060	**1097***	75	1240 - 1420	1330	**1328***	62	1510 - 1600	1600	**1563***	45
by location:												
Santa Monica Panel (*k*=4)	1060 - 1150	1060	**1085**	41	1240 - 1330	1330	**1305**	41	1510 - 1600	1600	**1560**	46
New York Panel (*k*=5)	970 - 1240	1150	**1107**	93	1240 - 1420	1330	**1346**	70	1510 - 1600	1600	**1565**	45
by task:												
Brain Boost (*k*=2)	1060 - 1150	1060	**1100**	47	1240 - 1330	1240	**1280**	47	1600	1600	**1600**	-
Crime (*k*=2)	1150 - 1240	1150	**1190**	47	1330 - 1420	1330	**1370**	47	1510 - 1600	1600	**1560**	47
Catfish (*k*=2)	1060 - 1150	1150	**1110**	47	1330 - 1420	1420	**1380**	47	1510 - 1600	1600	**1560**	47
Lake to River (*k*=2)	970 - 1060	970	**1010**	47	1240 - 1330	1240	**1280**	47	1510	1510	**1510**	-
Parks (NY only, *k*=1)	1060	1060	**1060**	-	1330	1330	**1330**	-	1600	1600	**1600**	-

*Suggested as final cut points for the standards.

Note: Number of panel members and number of groups are noted as n and k respectively.

E. SORTING RESULTS

Table E.1
Sorting Means and Standard Deviations

	Unsatisfactory/ Unacceptable		*Adequate/ Barely Acceptable*		*Proficient/ Clearly Acceptable*		*Exemplary/ Outstanding*	
	Mean	*SD*	*Mean*	*SD*	*Mean*	*SD*	*Mean*	*SD*
Freshmen								
Overall	876	175	1065	184	1302	162	1421	134
By location:								
Santa Monica	853	117	1083	195	1304	167	1405	140
New York	894	204	783	173	771	161	1435	129
By task:								
Brain Boost	798	101	1031	181	1272	155	1372	96
Crime	959	165	1074	190	1309	173	1475	152
Catfish	894	128	1094	188	1297	159	1339	161
Lake to River	877	236	1081	204	1324	185	1402	108
Parks (NY)	840	140	1047	149	1311	123	1526	88
Seniors								
Overall	866	140	1195	204	1410	187	1471	129
By location:								
Santa Monica	864	157	1170	215	1399	200	1442	143
New York	866	130	1216	194	1417	180	1506	102
By task:								
Brain Boost	849	184	1106	201	1416	221	1428	142
Crime	923	122	1210	204	1355	239	1439	123
Catfish	840	122	1199	205	1424	176	1568	60
Lake to River	861	137	1256	182	1402	154	1433	151
Parks (NY)	864	126	1257	201	1450	148	1510	104

F. FEEDBACK FORM MEANS AND STANDARD DEVIATIONS

Table F.1
Feedback Form Means and Standard Deviations

Questions About the Individual Standard-Setting Process	Mean	SD
How confident do feel about the standards you set?[a]	3.44	.67
Was it difficult to arrive at the standards? (yes = 1/no = 0)	.73	.45
Do you think your perspectives on the standards will be different from those of other panel members? (yes = 1/no = 0)	.63	.49
Questions About The Group Standard-Setting Process		
How confident do feel about the standards set by your group?[a]	3.83	.64
Was it difficult to arrive at consensus with the other panel members? (yes = 1/no = 0)	.22	.42
Were your perspectives on the standards different from those of other panel members? (yes = 1/no = 0)	.76	.43

[a] Rated on a scale from 1 to 5 where 1 = "not confident at all," 3 = "moderately confident" and 5 = "extremely confident" (points 3 and 4 on the scale were unlabeled).

REFERENCES

Angoff, W. H., "Scales, norms, and equivalent scores," in R. L. Thorndike (ed.), *Educational Measurement,* 2nd ed., Washington, D.C.: American Council on Education, 1971.

American Educational Research Association, American Psychological Association, and National Council on Measurement in Education (AERA, APA, and NCME), "Standards for educational and psychological testing." Washington, D.C.: American Psychological Association, 1999.

Berk, R. A., "A consumer's guide to setting performance standards on criterion-referenced tests," *Review of Educational Research,* Vol. 56, 1986, pp. 137–172.

Cizek, G. J., "Conjectures on the rise and fall of standard setting: An introduction to context and practice," in G. J. Cizek, (ed.), *Setting Performance Standards: Concepts, Methods, and Perspectives,* Mahwah, N.J.: Lawrence Erlbaum, 2001, pp. 1–17.

Cizek, G. J., "Standard-setting guidelines," *Educational Measurement: Issues and Practice,* Vol. 15, 1996b, pp. 13–21.

Cizek, G. J., M. B. Bunch, and H. Koons, "Setting performance standards: Contemporary methods," *Educational Measurement: Issues and Practice,* Winter 2004, pp. 31–50.

Collegiate Learning Assessment (CLA): Critical Thinking, Analytic Reasoning, Problem Solving, and Writing Skills: Definitions and Scoring Criteria. As of April 30, 2009: http://www.cae.org/content/pdf/CLA_Scoring%20Criteria.pdf

Ebel, R. L., *Essentials of Educational Measurement,* Englewood Cliffs, N.J.: Prentice-Hall, 1972.

Ennis, R. H., "Critical thinking assessment," *Theory into Practice*, Vol. 32, 1993, pp. 179–186.

Facione, P. A., *The California Critical Thinking Skills Test: College-level,* Technical Report #1 —Experimental Validation and Content Validity, ERIC Document ED 327-549, Millbrae, Calif.: The California Academic Press, 1990.

Facione, P. A., *Critical Thinking: What It Is and Why It Counts, Insight Assessment,* 2009, The California Academic Press, Update. As of July 13, 2009: http://www.insightassessment.com/pdf_files/what&why2006.pdf

Facione, P. A., N. C. Facione, and C. A. Giancarlo, "The disposition toward critical thinking: Its character, measurement, and relationship to critical thinking skill," *Informal Logic,* Vol. 20, 2000, pp. 61–84.

Faggen, J., *Setting Standards for Constructed-Response Tests: An Overview* (ETS RM-94-19), Princeton, N.J.: Educational Testing Service, 1994.

Fitzpatrick, A. R., "Social influences in standard setting: The effects of social interaction on group judgments," *Review of Educational Research,* Vol. 59, No. 3, Autumn, 1989, pp. 315–328.

Glass, G. V., "Standards and criteria," *Journal of Educational Measurement,* Vol. 15, 1978, pp. 237–261.

Hambleton, R. K., and B. S. Plake, "Using an extended Angoff procedure to set standards on complex performance assessments," *Applied Measurement in Education,* Vol. 8, 1995, pp. 41–55.

Hambleton, R. K., R. M. Jaeger, B. S. Plake, and C. Mills, "Setting performance standards on complex educational assessments," *Applied Psychological Measurement,* Vol. 24, 2000, pp. 355–366.

Hambleton, R. K., and M. J. Pitoniak, "Setting performance standards," in R. K. Hambleton and M. J. Pitoniak eds., *Educational Measurement,* Westport, Conn.: Praeger Publishers, 2006, pp. 433–470.

Hambleton, R. K., "Setting performance standards on educational assessments and criteria for evaluating the process," in G. J. Cizek, (ed.), *Setting Performance Standards: Concepts, Methods, and Perspectives,* Mahwah, N.J.: Lawrence Erlbaum, 2001, pp. 89–116.

Hersh, R. H., *Life Isn't a Multiple Choice Question*, Council for Aid to Education, 2006. As of June 1, 2009:
http://cae.org/content/pdf/HershLifeIsntAMultipleChoiceQuestion.pdf

Impara, J. C., and B. S. Plake, "Standard setting: An alternative approach," *Journal of Educational Measurement,* Vol. 34, 1997, pp. 353–366.

Jaeger, R. M., and C. N. Mills, "An integrated judgment procedure for setting standards on complex large-scale assessments," in G. J. Cizek, (ed.), *Setting Performance Standards: Concepts, Methods, and Perspectives,* Mahwah, N.J.: Lawrence Erlbaum, 2001, pp. 313–338.

Kane, M. T., "Validating performance standards associated with passing scores," *Review of Educational Research,* Vol. 64, 1994, pp. 425–461.

Kane, M. T., "So much remains the same: Conception and status of validation in setting standards," in G. J. Cizek (ed.), *Setting Performance Standards: Concepts, Methods and Perspectives,* Mahwah, N.J.: Erlbaum, 2001, pp. 53–88.

Kingston, N. M., S. R. Kahl, K. P. Sweeney, and L. Bay, "Setting performance standards using the body of work method," in G. J. Cizek, (ed.), *Setting Performance Standards: Concepts, Methods, and Perspectives,* Mahwah, N.J.: Lawrence Erlbaum, 2001, pp. 219–248.

Klein, S., "Establishing pass/fail standards," *The Bar Examiner,* Vol. 55, 1986, pp. 18–30.

Klein, S., "Setting pass/fail standards on constructed-response licensing tests," paper presented at the meetings of the National Council on Measurement in Education, Chicago, Ill., April 1991.

Klein, S., "How the CLA differs from NCLB," Council for Aid to Education, 2007. As of July 13, 2009:
http://www.cae.org/content/pdf/NCLBcomparisonSPK.pdf

Klein, S., D. Freedman, R. Shavelson, and R. Bolus, "Assessing school effectiveness," *Evaluation Review,* December 2008.

Klein, S., R. Shavelson, R. Benjamin, and R. Bolus, "The Collegiate Learning Assessment: Facts and fantasies," *Evaluation Review,* Vol. 31, 2007, pp. 415–439.

Kuhn, D., "A developmental model of critical thinking," *Educational Researcher,* Vol. 28, 1999, pp. 16–26.

Lewis, D. M., H. C. Mitzel, D. R. Green, and R. J. Patz, *The Bookmark Standard Setting Procedure,* Monterey, Calif.: McGraw-Hill, 1999.

Livingston, S. A., and M. J. Zieky, *Passing Scores: A Manual for Setting Standards of Performance on Educational and Occupational Tests,* Princeton, N.J.: Educational Testing Service, 1982.

Loomis, S. C., and M. L. Bourque, "From tradition to innovation: Standard Setting on the National Assessment of Educational Progress," in G. J. Cizek, (ed.), *Setting Performance Standards: Concepts, Methods, and Perspectives,* Mahwah, N.J.: Lawrence Erlbaum, 2001 pp. 175–217.

Mitzel, H. C., D. M. Lewis, R. J. Patz, and D. R. Green, "The Bookmark procedure: Psychological perspectives," in G. J. Cizek, (ed.), *Setting Performance Standards: Concepts, Methods, and Perspectives,* Mahwah, N.J.: Lawrence Erlbaum, 2001, pp. 249–281.

Nedelsky, L., "Absolute grading standards for objective tests," *Educational and Psychological Measurement,* Vol. 14, 1954, pp. 3–19.

Norris, S. P., "Can we test validly for critical thinking?" *Educational Researcher,* Vol. 18, 1989, pp. 21–26.

Plake, B. S., and R. K. Hambleton, "The analytic judgment method for setting standards on complex performance assessments," in G. J. Cizek (ed.), *Setting Performance Standards: Concepts, Methods, and Perspectives,* Hillsdale, NJ: Erlbaum, 2001, pp. 283–312.

Raymond, M. R., and J. B. Reid, "Who made thee a judge? Selecting and training Participants for standard setting," *Setting Performance Standards: Concepts, Methods, and Perspectives,* Mahwah, N.J.: Lawrence Erlbaum, 2001, pp. 119–157.

Watson, G., and E. M. Glaser, *Watson-Glaser Critical Thinking Appraisal,* Cleveland, OH: Psychological Corporation, 1980.

Zieky, M., "So much has changed: How the setting of cutscores has evolved since the 1980s," in G. J. Cizek, (ed.), *Setting Performance Standards: Concepts, Methods, and Perspectives,* Mahwah, N.J.: Lawrence Erlbaum, 2001, pp. 19–52.

Zieky, M., M. Perie, and S. Livingston, *A Primer on Setting Cut Scores on Tests of Educational Achievement,* Princeton, N.J.: Educational Testing Service, 2006.